Civil War
Williamsburg

Confederate and Union soldiers skirmish at the College of William and Mary around the battered statue of colonial governor Lord Botetourt.

Civil War
Williamsburg

By Carson O. Hudson, Jr.

PUBLISHED BY THE COLONIAL WILLIAMSBURG FOUNDATION
WILLIAMSBURG, VIRGINIA
IN ASSOCIATION WITH STACKPOLE BOOKS
MECHANICSBURG, PENNSYLVANIA

Published by The Colonial Williamsburg Foundation,
Williamsburg, Virginia, in association with Stackpole Books,
Mechanicsburg, Pennsylvania

Library of Congress Cataloging-in-Publication Data
Hudson, Carson O.
     Civil War Williamsburg / by Carson O. Hudson, Jr.
          p.   cm.
     Includes bibliographical references and index.
     ISBN 0-87935-163-2 (C.W.)
     ISBN 0-8117-2707-6 (Stackpole)
          1. Historic sites—Virginia—Williamsburg—Guidebooks.
     2. Williamsburg (Va.)—Guidebooks. 3. Virginia—History—Civil
     War, 1861–1865. I. Title.
     F234.W7H83 1997
     917.55'42520443—dc21   97-10557
                                                            CIP

Front cover: Don Troiani, *Rebel Yell* (detail)
Back cover: William McIlvaine, Jr., *Williamsburg Va May 9, 1862*

Book design: Ken Scaglia

This book was printed and bound in the United States of America

To Company C, Thirty-second Virginia Infantry,
the "Williamsburg Junior Guard," who went to war,
and to the men, women, and children,
both black and white, who remained behind.
Williamsburg was their town.

A scene from the Battle of Williamsburg.
Drawn on May 6, 1862.

Contents

Acknowledgments

I would like to thank the many people who assisted in the preparation of this volume. There were many opinions to ask, much research to be studied, and numerous original sources to be tracked down.

Linda Rowe and Kevin Kelly of the Colonial Williamsburg Research Department made themselves available for questions and direction. Lou Powers was especially helpful with information on Cynthia B. T. Coleman.

Liz Ackert and Gail Greve of the John D. Rockefeller, Jr. Library, Colonial Williamsburg, were most helpful in assisting my research and locating original volumes, papers, and manuscripts. Mary Keeling took much of the pain out of finding period photographs and prints and was a joy to work with.

Anne Marie Millar read and reread and then typed and retyped the manuscript, all the while offering constructive criticism. Thanks for the patience and encouragement.

Dennis Cotner and Les Jensen, both Civil War scholars and historians of the first quality, offered their advice and valuable information. Dennis was especially helpful with his knowledge of the local area and the preparation of the maps.

The late Peninsula historian Parke Rouse and Steve Elliott of the Colonial Williamsburg Foundation reviewed my earliest attempts and encouraged me to continue.

Ralee Durden, John Ogden, and Bradley Hayes of the Publications Department spent many hours confirming details and making innumerable copies of the manuscript and layout.

Ken Scaglia of Scaglia Studio created an elegant design in which to present the words and images of those who experienced civil war in Williamsburg.

Finally, Suzanne Coffman of the Publications Department introduced me to the vagaries (and timetables) of the publishing business. She assisted in polishing the work to make it presentable and reviewed the documentation with me to ensure the book's accuracy. Special thanks to her father for taking her to all those Civil War battlefields during her childhood, thus preparing her to edit this manuscript. To her and all the others, thank you.

Credits

The map of tidewater and central Virginia was prepared by Ken Scaglia. The maps of the Southeastern Virginia Peninsula, the Battle of Williamsburg, and Civil War sites in Williamsburg were prepared by Ken Scaglia based on maps by Dennis Cotner.

The Colonial Williamsburg Foundation gratefully acknowledges the permission of the following organizations and individuals to reproduce materials in their collections.

Mrs. Donald C. Adams, *George William Whitaker* (p. 91)

Mrs. Cynthia Barlowe, *Cynthia Beverley Tucker Coleman* (p. 58)

Civil War Library and Museum, Philadelphia, Pa.: *Williamsburg Va May 9, 1862* (back cover and p. 30)

College of William and Mary, Williamsburg, Virginia: *Robert Saunders* (p. 60, courtesy Muscarelle Museum of Art); *Program for the 1860 commencement* (p. 74; courtesy University Archives, Earl Gregg Swem Library)

Eastern State Hospital, Williamsburg, Virginia: *John Minson Galt II* (p. 69)

Library of Congress, Washington, D.C.: *Kearny at Battle of Williamsburg* (p. 10); *George B. McClellan* (p. 19); *Hooker's Division* (p. 23); *Hancock's Brigade* (p. 23); *Lieutenant George Armstrong Custer* (p. 41); *General William H. Payne* (p. 55); *The C. de Paris riding into Yorktown* (p. 85)

Museum of the Confederacy, Richmond, Virginia: *Flag of the Fifteenth Virginia Infantry* (p. 14; photo by Katherine Wetzel); *Mourning Badge* (p. 15; photo by Katherine Wetzel); *Joseph E. Johnston* (p. 19; courtesy the Eleanor S. Brockenbrough Library); *John Bankhead Magruder* (p. 19; courtesy the Eleanor S. Brockenbrough Library); *Benjamin S. Ewell* (p. 79; courtesy the Eleanor S. Brockenbrough Library)

National Archives and Records Administration, Washington, D.C.: *John Pelham* (p. 62)

New-York Historical Society, New York, N.Y.: *Wise's Last Raid* (pp. 2, 75); *Citizens with Umbrellas* (p. 22); *Negro Types* (p. 31); *Confederate Scout* (p. 31); *The Vest Mansion* (p. 45); *Listening to the Battle of Cold Harbor* (p. 50); *The Powder Horn* (p. 52); *Camp of Troop C* (p. 52); *Bruton Church* (p. 62); *Escaped from Libby* (p. 77); *Posting the Outer Pickets* (p. 78); *Neglected graveyard of the first settlers* (p. 81); *Watching for Confederate Ironclads* (p. 81); *In Fort Magruder* (p. 87); *Soldiers atop ridge* (p. 89)

Texas State Library, Austin, Texas: *D.U. Barziza* (p. 48; courtesy the Archives Division)

Don Troiani, Southbury, Conn.: *Rebel Yell* (front cover)

Virginia Historical Society, Richmond, Virginia: *Enemy Shelling Headquarters of Genl S.P. Heintzelman* (pp. 6, 26–27); *College and Street Scene* (p. 13); *View of "Fort Magruder"* (pp. 16–17); *The Battlefield of Williamsburg* (p. 25); *Head Quarters of 3rd. Army Corps* (pp. 28, 88)

General Philip Kearny at the Battle of Williamsburg.

Introduction

The evening of May 5, 1862, ended as the day had begun, with rain. It had been a difficult day for many, and for some, the last day. In and around the old colonial capital of Williamsburg, several thousand United States and Confederate soldiers had just engaged in a wet, confusing, and sometimes desperate battle. Hundreds of wounded were now coming in from the woods and fields surrounding the town, and every available space in Williamsburg became a hospital. In the second year of the rebellion of the Southern states against what they considered to be an unjust government, the national tragedy of civil war had come to Williamsburg.

From 1699, when the Virginia General Assembly moved the colony's government from Jamestown to Williamsburg, until 1780, when another assembly moved the capital to Richmond, the city of Williamsburg stood in the spotlight of history as the capital of Virginia. George Washington, Thomas Jefferson, Patrick Henry, and scores of others acted out their roles here and oversaw great events, revolution, and the founding of our nation.

From 1861 until 1865, Williamsburg shared in the great events of a second revolution, although in a smaller role. As proud and patriotic as any city at any time, Williamsburg suffered through a battle on its doorstep, followed by the humiliation of occupation by an enemy army for almost three years. The town did not forget for quite a while.

Today, thousands of Americans once again march through Williamsburg. They come from north and south, east and west, not to fight for or against something but to learn of America's birth. The Colonial Williamsburg Foundation has gone to great lengths to re-create the eighteenth-century capital of Virginia so that, as the Foundation's motto states, "The Future May Learn from the Past."

Civil War Williamsburg is intended to remember another, sadder past, one that is just as important in the story of how we came to be who we are today. For those who care to take a little extra time and dig a little deeper, beyond the colonial exteriors, groups of school children, and modern visitors, some of that past is still visible.

Wartime Williamsburg, 1861–1865

In 1780, the importance of Williamsburg seemed to be in its past. In that year, the capital of the state of Virginia was moved from Williamsburg to a small village farther up the James River, a town called Richmond. The purpose of this move was to provide the new state government with a safer and more central location.

With the departure of the legislature and the governor, Williamsburg settled into a period of slumber. The town became known as a quiet and sleepy place with decaying buildings, a college, and a lunatic asylum. Thus Williamsburg entered the nineteenth century, a ghost of its former self.

What was Williamsburg like in 1860, just before the Civil War? Certainly it bore little similarity to its eighteenth-century past, and even less to its modern counterpart.

Geographically, the street names were different. Duke of Gloucester Street was known as Main Street, and the parallel streets were spoken of as "the back streets." Jamestown and Richmond Roads were known as Mill Road and Stage Road, respectively. At the east end of town, Waller Street was called Gallows Street, and the road that ran out of town toward Yorktown and Hampton, today named York Street, was known as Woodpecker Street.

If we were to travel back to 1860, we would enter the town from the east on Woodpecker Street. Standing on Main Street and looking west toward the College of William and Mary, we would see a quite

College and street scene. Drawn by David Henderson, a Confederate soldier, in early 1862.

(*Opposite*) Williamsburg, 1859–1860, looking east down Duke of Gloucester Street (Main Street) from the Wren Building.

Flag of the Fifteenth Virginia Infantry, made from the bridal gown of Catherine Heth Morrison.

different scene from that which greets us today. There were no paved streets and no lights. It would surprise us that the "sidewalks," such as they were, were also of dirt and overhung by shade trees, and that cattle grazed at will through the town. In the town as a whole, we would find no express office or railroad, no telegraph office, no banks, and no public school. There were nine private schools. They were the College of William and Mary, the Male Academy, the Female Institute or Academy, the Classical and Mathematical Institute, Mrs. Young's Female Academy, Mrs. Allen's Male and Female School, Mr. Blain's Mathematical and Classical School for Boys, Miss Lindsay's Academy, and Miss Gilliam's Seminary. The town also supported a newspaper, the *Weekly Gazette and Eastern Virginia Advertiser,* which is still published today as the *Virginia Gazette.*

The 1860 Census for Williamsburg (both free and slave schedules) listed a total of 1,895 persons residing in the city limits or at the lunatic asylum, of whom about two-fifths, or 743, were slaves. Most of those listed on the free schedule were native-born Americans, with only 17 foreign-born persons noted. The leading citizens of the town were doctors and lawyers, gentleman farmers and prosperous merchants. There were 134 persons listed as owning real estate and personal property valued at $1,000 or more. Of these, at least 22 were women who were heads of households or widows, and 3 were free blacks or mulattoes.

Most of the slaves in town were listed as house servants. Field slaves, laborers, and tradesmen tended to live on the farms and plantations outside the town. Slaves who resided in Williamsburg usually lived with their masters' households. They were forced to work most of the week but were allowed Sunday afternoons to go around the town. There appears to have been a curfew of nine o'clock.

Mourning badge worn by the ladies of Williamsburg upon the death of Stonewall Jackson.

Any slave or free black on the streets after this hour without permission could be whipped. A whipping post was located in the ravine across Francis Street, near what is now the tunnel entrance to the modern Colonial Parkway. Masters of slaves caught out after curfew were fined one dollar to collect their property. Slave traders operated in Williamsburg before the war, and there was a slave block on Market Square for auctions.

Slaves could accompany their masters to worship on Sundays at Bruton Parish Church, Williamsburg Baptist Church, or other churches. After 1855, there was the African Baptist Church, also known as the First Baptist Church, colored. There were no black schools; the education of slaves was illegal under state law. Evidence indicates, however, that this prohibition was ignored by some masters who tutored their slaves.

Williamsburg's lethargy was disturbed in April 1861, when Virginia passed an ordinance of secession, leaving the United States and throwing her fate in with the states of the deep South in the new Southern Confederacy. On May 23, E. H. Lively, publisher of the *Weekly Gazette and Eastern Virginia Advertiser,* raised the town's first secessionist flag over his mother's house, where the paper was published.

Like most able-bodied Virginians, the men of the town, including the students, professors, and even the president of the College of William and Mary, volunteered for military service. The faculty minutes of the college for May 10, 1861, state:

> Whereas—Civil war is imminent, and the state of Virginia is threatened with an armed invasion; and whereas the exposed position of this section of the state requires that every citizen should be free to enlist in its defense; and whereas, a large majority of the students have already left college, and those who still remain—most of whom propose to leave—are unable, from the excited state of the public mind, to pursue their collegiate duties with profit—Therefore—Resolved—that the

exercises of the college be suspended during the remainder of the present session.

Over 90 percent of the student body joined the Confederate army, as opposed to only 50 percent who took up arms during the American Revolution.

Williamsburg's women proved just as fierce, if not more so, in their devotion to the Confederacy and their hatred of the dreaded "Yankees." As soldiers from other Southern states arrived in town to begin forming an army, the women tended the sick and opened their homes to the young volunteers. They prepared rations for the town's hospitals and sponsored balls and entertainments for the soldiers in the area. The ladies of the hospital located in the Female Academy presented a flag to Coppens's Zouaves from Louisiana, and Mrs. Catherine H. Morrison, the wife of a professor at the college, presented a flag made from her silk bridal gown to the Fifteenth Virginia Infantry. A ladies' "gunboat society" was formed for the purpose of raising funds to purchase a Confederate warship.

Fort Magruder, the road to Williamsburg, and the town in the distance. Drawn the day after the Battle of Williamsburg.

Many of the town's African-Americans supported the Southern war effort in other ways, such as becoming cooks or conscripted laborers for the army. Captain Octavius Coke, a Williamsburg lawyer, took his slave, W. B. Nelson, to war with him as a personal servant, as did Private Thomas J. Barlow, a student who enlisted from the college.

With secession, the state began to make preparations to defend itself from invasion. General Robert E. Lee, commander of Virginia's military effort in the early days of the war, understood that the tidewater Peninsula, flanked by both the York and James Rivers, could easily be used for an advance on the capital at Richmond. With this in mind, a series of forts and redoubts was planned and construction begun.

From May 1861 until March 1862, Confederate soldiers, hired free blacks, and rented slaves labored to make three defensive lines across the Peninsula. Upon its completion, the Williamsburg line was composed of a large earthen fort with supporting redoubts stretching across the peninsular approaches.

Fort Magruder, which was about two miles southeast of Williamsburg, was the principal Confederate defense of Williamsburg

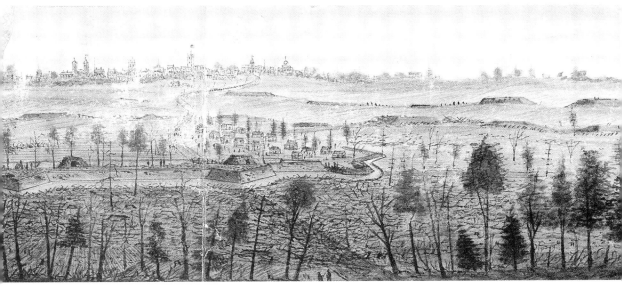

and commanded the main road leading toward Richmond. Named in honor of the Confederate area commander, General "Prince" John Bankhead Magruder, the fort was an elongated pentagon with walls fifteen feet high and nine feet thick surrounded by a moat nine feet deep. Toward the York River nine smaller redoubts were constructed. Southward toward the James River were five more. These were augmented by five additional forts and gun emplacements on Jamestown Island, one grandly called "Fort Pocahontas," about five miles from Williamsburg. The Jamestown Island batteries would protect the James River approaches to Richmond.

This defensive line was never fully used as intended, but Confederate troops occupied and defended part of it during the Confederate retreat from Yorktown and the subsequent Battle of Williamsburg. Following that battle, Fort Magruder (retaining its Confederate name) became the central defensive position for the occupying U.S. forces in the area and remained in Federal hands until their departure in September 1865.

Today the remains of Fort Magruder occupy a small park alongside Penniman Road outside the Williamsburg city limits. Owned by the United Daughters of the Confederacy, the property is marked with a monument erected by the citizens of Williamsburg on the one hundredth anniversary of the Battle of Williamsburg, May 5, 1962. The grounds have been fenced off to protect what still exists of the earthworks. Other redoubts of the original defensive line still remain, some still preserved, along the Colonial Parkway, on Colonial Williamsburg property, and on Jamestown Island.

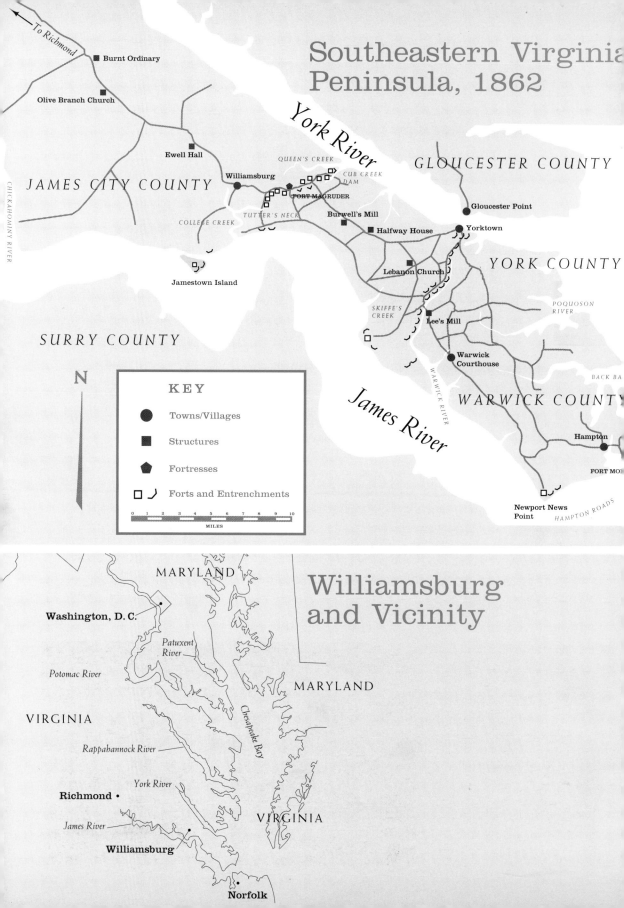

Southeastern Virginia Peninsula, 1862

To Richmond

Burnt Ordinary

Olive Branch Church

Ewell Hall

CHICKAHOMINY RIVER

JAMES CITY COUNTY

Williamsburg

York River

QUEEN'S CREEK

CUB CREEK DAM

FORT MAGRUDER

TUTTER'S NECK

COLLEGE CREEK

Jamestown Island

Burwell's Mill

Halfway House

GLOUCESTER COUNTY

Gloucester Point

Yorktown

Lebanon Church

YORK COUNTY

POQUOSON RIVER

SKIFFE'S CREEK

Lee's Mill

SURRY COUNTY

Warwick Courthouse

WARWICK RIVER

James River

WARWICK COUNTY

BACK BA

Hampton

FORT MO

Newport News Point

HAMPTON ROADS

KEY

● Towns/Villages

■ Structures

⬟ Fortresses

□ ⌐ Forts and Entrenchments

N

0 1 2 3 4 5 6 7 8 9 10
MILES

Williamsburg and Vicinity

MARYLAND

Washington, D.C.

Patuxent River

Potomac River

MARYLAND

VIRGINIA

Rappahannock River

Chesapeake Bay

York River

Richmond •

James River

VIRGINIA

Williamsburg •

Norfolk •

The Battle of Williamsburg

Since the Confederate victory at Manassas in July 1861, the two amateur armies in the east had watched one another in northern Virginia. Each sat blocking the path to its capital and waited. In early 1862, however, the strategic situation changed. General George B. McClellan, commander of the Union Army of the Potomac, conceived a new plan of attack. He would take a majority of his army from northern Virginia down the Potomac River to the Chesapeake Bay, then march up the tidewater Peninsula to capture Richmond in a lightning campaign. McClellan planned to enter through Richmond's "backdoor." Sitting astride the only road up the Peninsula, Williamsburg found itself once again at the forefront of national events as Federal troops converged on Fort Monroe in Hampton to begin their advance toward the new Confederate capital at Richmond.

The campaign began in March with the arrival of the first elements of McClellan's army at Fort Monroe. To counter the Union move, the Confederate army under General Joseph E. Johnston began the process of shifting to meet this new threat. A small force of Confederate troops had been on the Peninsula since early 1861, but with the appearance of General McClellan, this "Army of the Peninsula" found itself vastly outnumbered. The theatrics of General Magruder, however, stalled McClellan at the crucial moment. By marching and countermarching his troops across the Peninsula, Magruder convinced the overcautious McClellan that he confronted a much larger force. Before McClellan could react, he was facing the main Rebel army, freshly arrived from north of Richmond. Blocked now before Yorktown, General McClellan settled in to take the small port town by siege, just as the American army had done eighty-one years before against the British.

(Left to right) Confederate General Joseph E. Johnston. Union General George B. McClellan (detail). Confederate General John Bankhead Magruder (detail).

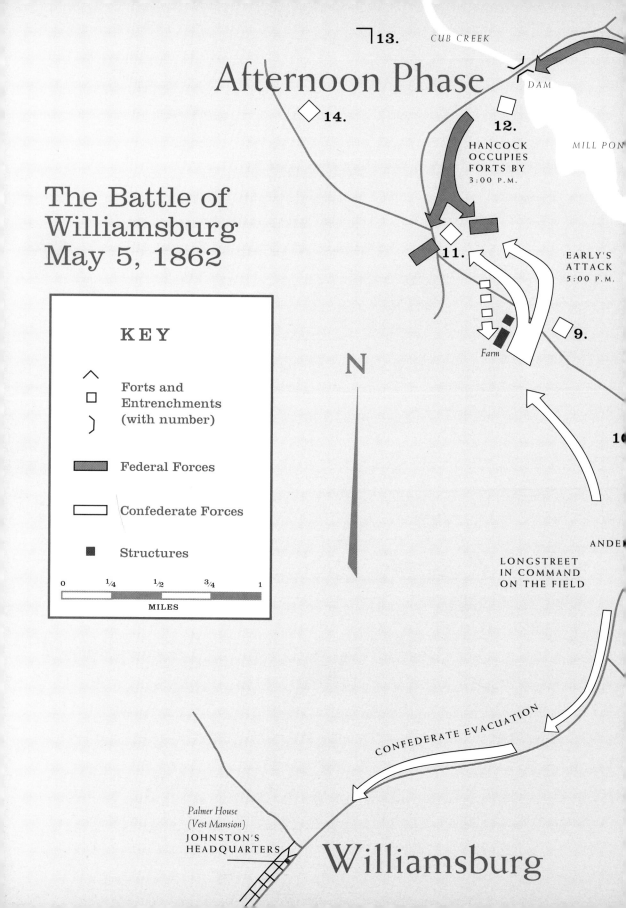

Afternoon Phase

⌐ **13.**   *CUB CREEK*

◇ **14.**

**The Battle of
Williamsburg
May 5, 1862**

DAM

□ **12.**

MILL PON

HANCOCK
OCCUPIES
FORTS BY
3:00 P.M.

◇ **11.**

EARLY'S
ATTACK
5:00 P.M.

◇ **9.**

Farm

N

1

KEY

⋀
□   Forts and
)   Entrenchments
    (with number)

▬▬ Federal Forces

▭▭ Confederate Forces

■   Structures

| 0 | ¼ | ½ | ¾ | 1 |
MILES

ANDE

LONGSTREET
IN COMMAND
ON THE FIELD

CONFEDERATE EVACUATION

*Palmer House
(Vest Mansion)*
JOHNSTON'S
HEADQUARTERS

Williamsburg

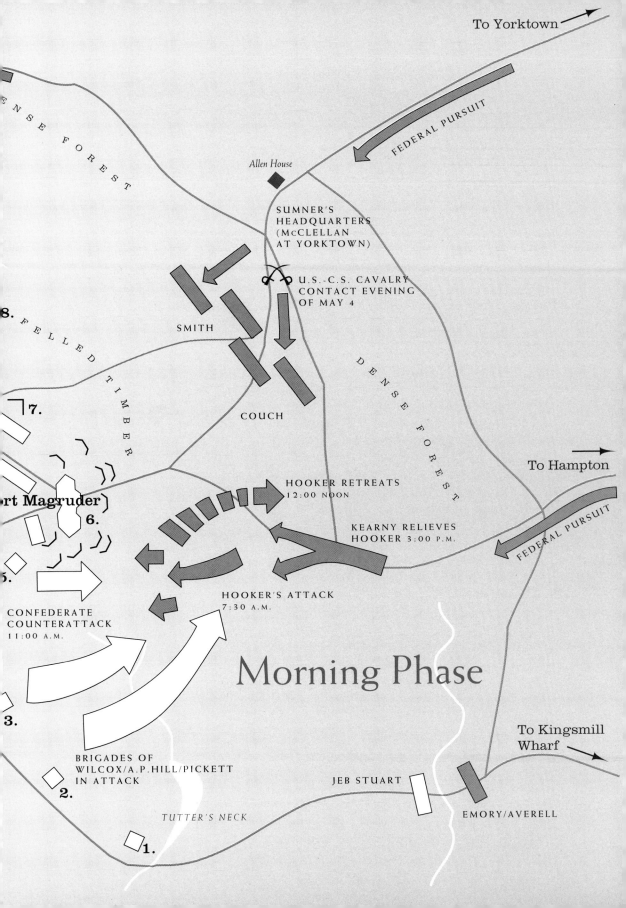

To Yorktown

FEDERAL PURSUIT

Allen House

SUMNER'S
HEADQUARTERS
(McCLELLAN
AT YORKTOWN)

U.S.-C.S. CAVALRY
CONTACT EVENING
OF MAY 4

8. FELLED TIMBER

SMITH

COUCH

DENSE FOREST

DENSE FOREST

7.

To Hampton

rt Magruder

6.

HOOKER RETREATS
12:00 NOON

KEARNY RELIEVES
HOOKER 3:00 P.M.

FEDERAL PURSUIT

5.

CONFEDERATE
COUNTERATTACK
11:00 A.M.

HOOKER'S ATTACK
7:30 A.M.

3.

Morning Phase

To Kingsmill
Wharf

BRIGADES OF
WILCOX/A.P.HILL/PICKETT
IN ATTACK

2.

JEB STUART

EMORY/AVERELL

TUTTER'S NECK

1.

Residents of Williamsburg observing the battle outside their town, May 5, 1862. Drawn by David Cronin of the First New York Mounted Rifles. Cronin was provost marshal in Williamsburg in 1864.

But General Johnston and his approximately 57,000 Confederate troops were not about to be besieged by McClellan and his 112,000 men. Holding his lines to the last moment, Johnston pulled his army into a retreat just as the Federals were preparing their assault. His objective was to find a better defensive position somewhere closer to Richmond. There, perhaps on the Chickahominy River, the Confederates would find more favorable ground and maybe reinforcements.

Initially the Rebels slipped away from Yorktown unnoticed, but soon the Union commanders found the enemy gone. General McClellan, in his own inimitable way, proclaimed a brilliant success and immediately ordered his cavalry in pursuit, followed by infantry. The rapidly advancing Federal cavalry caught up with the slowly moving Confederate rear guard just outside the city of Williamsburg.

On the afternoon of May 4, a cavalry fight developed just east of the town. The pursuing Union commander, General George Stoneman, halted his men to await infantry support. It arrived during the night, along with the rain.

Realizing that his army and transport wagons would require more time to evacuate toward Richmond, General Johnston made a decision on Monday morning, May 5, 1862. The approaching Union army was coming by way of two roads that converged just east of Williamsburg. Johnston ordered the division of General James Longstreet to turn about from the retreat and to occupy the defensive works that controlled the road. While Johnston proceeded on with the main body, Longstreet's forces would make a stand to block pursuit by the Union army and gain time for the Rebel troops.

A confused engagement began as General Longstreet's Confederates from Virginia, Florida, Mississippi, and Alabama battled with Union men from New York, New Hampshire, New Jersey, and Michigan. The combat was characterized by several hours of charge and countercharge, rain, and slippery mud. Soon, nearly 10,000 Confederates were holding and driving about 9,000 Union soldiers.

At this point, it was discovered that in the confusion the Rebels had not manned the entire defensive line. Several earthworks north of the evolving battle were empty and could be used to flank the Confederates. Union General Winfield Scott Hancock quickly seized the position and requested reinforcements to exploit his advantage. He waited in vain. General McClellan had not yet arrived on the field from Yorktown. Without an overall commander, indecision mired the Union troops as effectively as the mud.

Realizing he was in danger of being flanked, General Longstreet called upon reserve Confederate troops being held in Williamsburg. The brigade of General Jubal Early marched through the town and deployed to meet the new Union threat. It was growing dark as fresh Confederate soldiers assaulted the earthworks now held by Hancock. The attack was shattered with heavy casualties and the Confederates withdrew, pursued a short distance by a Federal countercharge.

Finally, as the firing died out for the day, General McClellan arrived on the field, too late to be of assistance. In his own mind, however, he had rallied his troops. McClellan wrote to his wife:

> I found everybody discouraged, officers and men; our troops in wrong positions, on the wrong side of the woods; no system, no cooperation, no orders give, roads blocked up. As soon as I came upon the field the men cheered like fiends, and I saw at once that I could save the day.

Battlefield artist Alfred Waud sketched these two views of the Battle of Williamsburg for Northern newspapers. The upper image depicts General Joseph Hooker's division engaging the Confederates. The lower shows General Winfield Scott Hancock's brigade.

Both sides claimed a victory. McClellan indeed had held the field, but the Confederates had delayed the pursuit. It is interesting to consider the respective views of the opposing commanders, each given the day after the battle:

Williamsburg, May 6, 1862

Hon. E. M. Stanton
Secretary of War.

Every hour proves our victory more complete. Enemy's Loss great; especially in officers. Have just heard of five more of their guns captured. Prisoners constantly arriving.

Geo. B. McClellan, Major-General, Commanding.

General Orders, Hdqrs. Dept. Northern Virginia, May 6, 1862

The commanding general announces to the Army an important success achieved yesterday in the repulse of the enemy's attacks upon the position of our rear guard near Williamsburg and the driving his forces to the woods by the troops of Major-Generals Longstreet and Hill, and Brigadier-General Stuart, commanded by the former. He congratulates those engaged upon the honors they have won, and offers them the thanks of the Army for their admirable conduct. . . .

By command of General Johnston

In the coming years, when one could look back at the Battles of Sharpsburg, Gettysburg, the Wilderness, and Cold Harbor, the action at Williamsburg would be remembered more as a large skirmish than as a major battle. But it served its purpose at the time, bloodying raw recruits and teaching them to work together. It taught Northerners and Southerners how to kill one another.

The citizens of Williamsburg witnessed war firsthand as the town became an immense hospital for the wounded and dying. Although Williamsburg was the location of the first military hospital in the Confederacy, the city was woefully unprepared for the battle that occurred on its doorstep. With more than 1,500 Southern soldiers killed, wounded, and missing, every available space in the town was used to treat the casualties. A Confederate civilian organization, the Richmond Ambulance Committee, had thirty-nine ambulances on the field the day of the battle. Even with this number, when the Confederates evacuated the city the next day, roughly 400 of the more seriously wounded had to be left behind. Some Confederate surgeons remained with the wounded, and private physicians joined them. The citizens of the town opened their doors and offered their homes as hospital space.

The Union army found the town full of yellow hospital flags. In addition to bringing in their own wounded, Federal authorities began

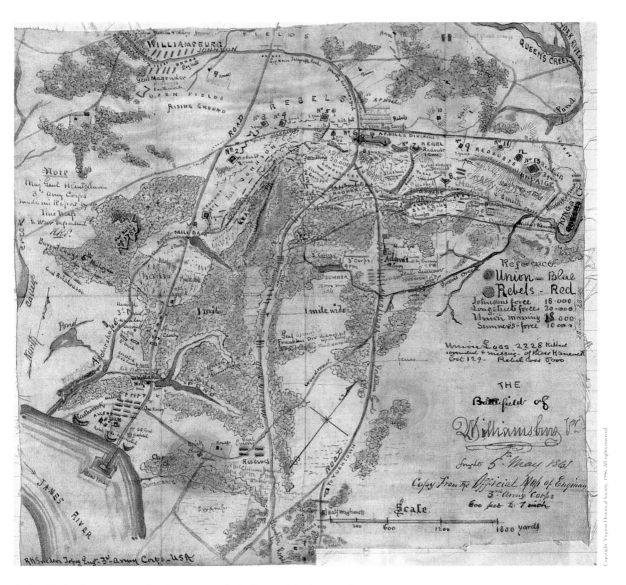

Robert K. Sneden, a topographical engineer with the Union's Third Army Corps, was an eyewitness to the Battle of Williamsburg. Sneden kept a visual record of his experiences during the Civil War. Some 30 of these artworks were published after the war, but the remaining 370—including watercolors of Fort Magruder, the Battle of Williamsburg, and scenes around Williamsburg after the battle—disappeared from public view. Sneden's nephew had inherited the works and used them as collateral for a loan upon which he ultimately defaulted. The bank sold the collection, and the images remained in private hands until 1993, when the Virginia Historical Society acquired them.

Sneden based his rendering of *The Battlefield of Williamsburg* on the army engineer's official map.

ENEMY SHELLING HEADQUARTERS OF Gen' S.P. Heintz

during the B

The Rebels crossed the Ravine at this tr
Webber's 53 att

commanding 3ʳᵈ Army Corps. at The ADAMS HOUSE

WILLIAMSBURG Vᵃ.

3. PM

...ed and broke the Union Line and Captured 2 guns of
...ould not carry them off.

(large plan of Battle.)

Sneden drew this scene from the Battle
of Williamsburg on May 6, the day after
the battle.

Wagons and clerks camped in Yard
Brick Seminary used as hospital   D.r Mercer's Office   D.r Mercer House   House was deserted
for union wounded   used for Adjt Genls office   used by Genl and staff   by all occupants

This watercolor shows the view looking
west from Waller Street. The Capitol
site, where the Female Academy was serving as a hospital for Union wounded,
is to the left.

collecting and sorting prisoners and gathering the dead. Several civilian surgeons were on the field through the offices of the United States Sanitary Commission, and there was embalming equipment available for the Federal dead. At least one woman, disguised as a man, was present. Sarah Emma Edmonds, known to her companions as "Franklin Thompson," served in the Second Michigan Infantry and assisted the military surgeons with their work the night of the battle.

The medical director of the Army of the Potomac, Charles S. Tripler, reported that there were about 700 wounded Federal soldiers and 333 wounded Confederates in the town. The remainder of the wounded, including an additional 100 wounded prisoners, were attended to in various field depots near the James and York Rivers. Several Federal government and Sanitary Commission steam transports were employed near Queen's Creek on the York River to transport the wounded of both sides to Fort Monroe. Most of the wounded and prisoners seem to have been removed by May 12, a week after the battle. At least 60 Confederates who were too badly wounded to be moved remained under Federal supervision in Williamsburg.

Williamsburg found itself an occupied city. In an irony of history and as a hollow echo of its past, the Federal army bands paraded up Duke of Gloucester Street (Main Street) playing "Yankee Doodle."

Federal and Confederate surgeons at work after the Battle of Williamsburg.

Federal Occupation

Throughout the remainder of the war, Williamsburg lived under martial law and had the dubious distinction of being the "border" between United States authority and the Confederacy. The city endured raids by Confederates and reconnaissances by Union cavalry. Newspapers and mail from both sides were exchanged through the town. Intelligence, both official and unofficial, traveled through Williamsburg to the North and the South.

Union wagons rumbled down Duke of Gloucester Street. Within a week of the Battle of Williamsburg, Federal forces erected telegraph lines in the city. The Fifth Pennsylvania Cavalry confiscated the presses of the local newspaper, the *Weekly Gazette and Eastern Virginia Advertiser.* The Pennsylvanians began their own paper, the *Cavalier,* which proclaimed, "The Union forever, and freedom to all."

Soon after the Union troops arrived, the newly appointed military governor, Colonel David Campbell of the Fifth Pennsylvania Cavalry, arrested several prominent citizens and dispatched them under guard to Norfolk. There the Union district commander, General Henry M. Naglee, soon released them on the technical grounds that there could be no material charge against peaceful citizens and that, because of age or profession (one was a physician), they were considered exempt from military duty.

After this incident, city residents were permitted to remain in Williamsburg unmolested as long as they caused no difficulty for the military authorities. This state of affairs, however, did not mean that the townspeople accepted their occupation gracefully. The women of Williamsburg sometimes went out of their way to ignore, taunt, or snub Federal soldiers and their flag. Not all of the invaders were found to be offensive, though. In 1863, one young lady of the town fell in love with the acting provost marshal, Sergeant John Fisher, and convinced him to desert to the Confederacy.

With the Federal occupation, many slaves simply disappeared, and several residents complained of their flight. One African-American who remained, Eliza Baker, remembered many years later that she was surprised that the first "Yankee" she met didn't have horns, as she had been forewarned by her mistress.

With the issuing of the Emancipation Proclamation in 1863, slavery ceased to exist in the town. A few blacks remained loyal to past masters and mistresses, whereas others hired themselves out or departed for greener pastures. Three black residents, Til, a cook, Jake, her husband, and Yellow Jim, a gardener, are known to have spied for the Confederacy. Some African-Americans joined the United States Army to fight against their former masters. At least two regiments of United States Colored Troops, the Sixth United States Colored Infantry and

Union wagons on Duke of Gloucester Street four days after the Battle of Williamsburg. The steeple of Bruton Parish Church shows above the trees on the right, and the Wren Building appears at the end of the street. Telegraph lines have already been strung on the right side of the roadway.

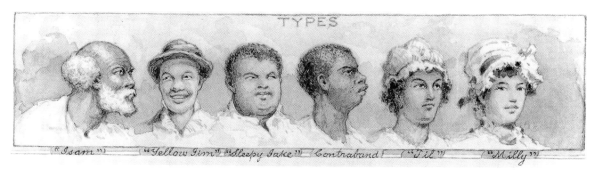

TYPES

"Isam"   "Yellow Jim"   "Sleepy Jake"   "Contraband!"   "Jil"   "Milly"

the First United States Colored Cavalry, were quartered near the town in 1864. Toward the end of the war, black children were being educated in the basement of the Williamsburg Baptist Church, and the Freedmen's Bureau arrived in 1865 to assist blacks in adjusting to a free society. A Quaker mission and school were established in 1866 at Fort Magruder by the "Friends' Association of Philadelphia and Its Vicinity for the Relief of the Colored Freedmen."

Although the main Confederate armies in Virginia were engaged elsewhere after May 1862, there was "partisan," or guerilla, activity in the Williamsburg area throughout the war. Confederate infantry and cavalry under General Henry A. Wise, a former governor of Virginia, attempted to harass and ambush Federal cavalry pickets and patrols whenever possible. On at least three occasions, there were serious Confederate raids on the city itself, the most significant attack occurring on the morning of September 9, 1862. Confederate cavalry swept into Williamsburg, and a short skirmish on the grounds of the College of William and Mary resulted in six Union soldiers killed and fifteen wounded. That afternoon, in apparent retaliation, drunken Federal troops set fire to the college's main building.

In February 1863, the Federal provost marshal, Major Christopher Kleinz, suspended services at Bruton Parish Church because of disloyal utterances made by the rector, Thomas M. Ambler. Then, in late March, there was an aborted attempt by the Confederates to attack Fort Magruder. Retreating Rebels found themselves involved in a street battle on Duke of Gloucester Street (Main Street) as they tried to leave the town. Captain Gustavus A. Wallace of Company F, Fifty-ninth Virginia Infantry, wrote of his company's actions:

> I then determined to make my way through Williamsburg . . . and was proceeding over the open field toward the town when we were approached by a body of cavalry on our left. I immediately formed line of battle and advanced at double quick speed in good order. They seeming to advance, I halted and fired several rounds. Having dispersed them, I marched by the flank to the town. Another large body of cavalry in the meantime was discovered in a field on our left who followed us to the town.

(*Top*) African-Americans of wartime Williamsburg. Drawn by David Cronin.

(*Above*) A Confederate scout near Williamsburg. Drawn by David Cronin.

When I struck the main street up which I posted my force, this last body followed. In the meantime we captured four prisoners, horses arms, and etc. and fired on several who would not surrender. I then discovered about 30 or 40 cavalry arriving ahead of us at College Place. Having thus the enemy to contend with at each end of the street, I formed my men on the right side of Main Street, when the body at the College advanced in a charge. We held our fire until they were close to us. Our fire broke and confused them. We killed three men at this fire and wounded several. . . . I continued to move but made another stand at the college. . . . We did not lose a man.

Services at Bruton Parish Church were suspended during the occupation.

In response to this last skirmish, during which it was believed that residents exchanged food and information with Confederate soldiers, the following general order was published:

Gen. Order No. 1   Fourth Army Corps.
                                    Yorktown, Va.
                                    Mar. 29th, 1863

Commanding Officer Williamsburg, Va.

The attack of the enemy on our lines this Sabbath morning was accompanied by circumstances of so aggravated a character as to call for prompt and severe punishment to those most implicated. Conclusive evidence has been furnished to the Commanding General that the attack was aided if not planned by citizens of Williamsburg, and carried to a successful end by them and their abettors outside the lines: that the enemy were led into the city by one or more citizens, and when once in, they were enabled by the aid of the citizens and their own overwhelming force to occupy the most advantageous points for attack and defence: that upon their occupation of the city, they were assisted by the citizens in their attack upon our forces, who were fired upon from the houses lining the streets, the dead bodies of the murdered being despoiled and stripped, their boots pulled off their feet; that the stores of their sympathizers within the city were thrown open to their advantage and their horses loaded with sacks prepared for their arrival.

To provide against a repetition of the outrage the commanding General directs:

1st—That all privileges to all storekeepers in the city of Williamsburg and vicinity to purchase and sell goods are revoked.

2nd—That all citizens who are willing to take the oath of allegiance to the Government of the United States will present themselves to the Provost Marshall of Williamsburg for the purpose of taking such oath on or before April 1st, 1863.

3rd—That all citizens in the city of Williamsburg and vicinity who are not willing to take the oath of allegiance to the Government of the United States, excepting the servants and employes of the Eastern Lunatic Asylum of the State of Virginia, will prepare themselves and their families to be placed beyond the lines now occupied by the armed forces of the said govt. by April 2nd, 1863.

4th—the greatest publicity possible will be given to this order and the cause leading to its issue and the end to be accomplished by its enforcement will be communicated to all concerned.

Issuance of this general order caused great concern not only among residents of the city but also among higher Union authorities. Since the town was populated mostly with older men, women, children, and those African-American servants who had remained, it would have proven a cruelty to enforce. Consequently, the general order was revoked the following day and replaced by a new directive:

> Headquarters Dept. of Va.
> 7th Army Corps.
> Fort Monroe, March 31st, 1863.

Maj. Gen. E.D. Keyes
Comdg. Yorktown, Va.
General:
In view of the raid on Williamsburg on Sunday last, and rumors of complicity on the part of the inhabitants with the assailants, you will give orders as follows:

1st—No persons shall be allowed to go to Williamsburg from any point South of Fort Magruder without taking the oath of allegiance.

2nd—No citizen of Williamsburg will be permitted to go to Yorktown from any point south of Fort Magruder without taking the oath of allegiance.

3rd—No person will be allowed to trade in Williamsburg without first taking the oath of allegiance.

4th—No further supplies will be allowed to be taken to Williamsburg for the use of the inhabitants, except the produce of the neighboring farms, until further orders. An investigation will be made into the circumstances alleged to have occurred at the time of the attack and if the parties accused of aiding and abetting it and reasonable presumption of their guilt is shown, they will be brought before a military tribunal and punished according to the laws of war.

> JOHN A. DIX
> Maj. General

In 1864, the Williamsburg area served as part of the staging area for Union General Benjamin Butler's ill-fated Bermuda Hundred Campaign, in which his 39,000-man Army of the James attempted to slip into Richmond's backdoor. Also in 1864, Williamsburg witnessed the end of Union General Judson Kilpatrick's failed raid on Richmond. Returning Federal cavalrymen paraded down Duke of Gloucester Street. An observer noted:

> Some of the gayer troopers wore conspicuous regalia, made up of civilian apparel, spoils taken not for their value but in the spirit of wanton mischief. One had adorned his horse with net armor made out of a hoop skirt; another wore a lady's "skoop-bonnet" with a huge bow. A large number wore stove pipe beaver hats of antique models, piling them up one upon another. One boasted of having a tower of eight telescoped in this style and waggishly asserted that the top one was "Jeff Davis's Sunday-go-to-meeting hat."

The last military action around the city occurred at about 3 A.M. February 11, 1865, as eight members of Colonel John S. Mosby's Forty-third Virginia Cavalry Battalion swept into the eastern part of the town. On a scouting mission of the Williamsburg area, the Confederate horsemen overran a picket post. The Southerners suffered no casualties themselves but did kill one Union soldier, wound four others, and capture four more. After causing a great deal of early morning confusion, the raiders quickly withdrew from the town.

With the surrender of General Lee at Appomattox in April 1865, an uneasy but welcome peace returned to Virginia and Williamsburg. Ex-Confederate soldiers and refugee residents returned to begin their lives anew. The city continued to be occupied, and Virginia became Federal Military District Number 1 as Reconstruction began. Federal troops finally left the city in September 1865, and one of the darkest periods of the town's existence began to fade into the past. It would not be until the twentieth century that the city would fully recover.

Civil War Sites in Williamsburg

This section lists the significant sites of the Williamsburg area and their associations with the Civil War. The selected sites run generally from the eastern end of the modern city to the west, which follows the progression of the Union armies in their advance on Richmond in 1862. The modern names of buildings and sites have been given first, with each site's 1860s name or identification following in parentheses.

Civil War Sites in Williamsburg

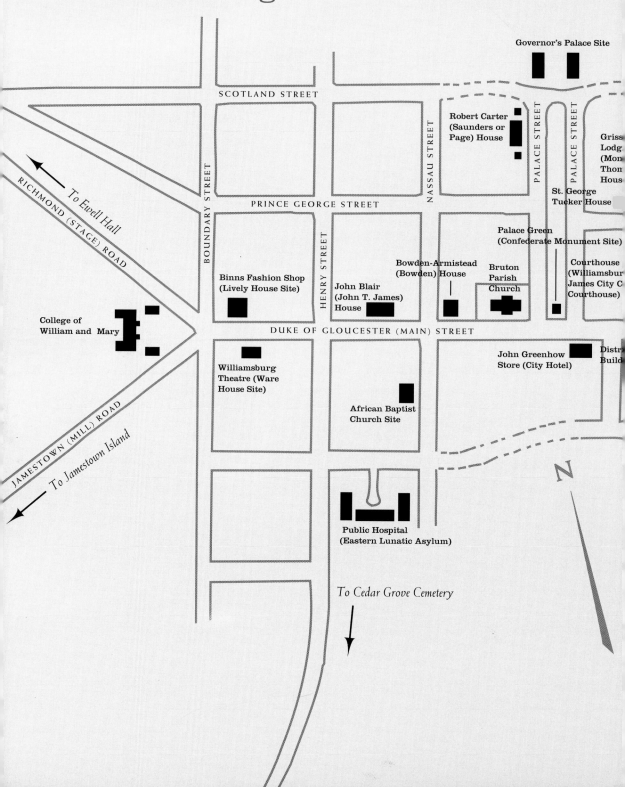

Governor's Palace Site

SCOTLAND STREET

Robert Carter
(Saunders or
Page) House

Griss...
Lodg...
(Mon...
Thon...
Hous...

St. George
Tucker House

NASSAU STREET

PALACE STREET

PALACE STREET

To Ewell Hall

RICHMOND (STAGE) ROAD

PRINCE GEORGE STREET

BOUNDARY STREET

Palace Green
(Confederate Monument Site)

HENRY STREET

Bowden-Armistead
(Bowden) House

Bruton
Parish
Church

Courthouse
(Williamsbur...
James City C...
Courthouse)

Binns Fashion Shop
(Lively House Site)

John Blair
(John T. James)
House

College of
William and Mary

DUKE OF GLOUCESTER (MAIN) STREET

Williamsburg
Theatre (Ware
House Site)

African Baptist
Church Site

John Greenhow
Store (City Hotel)

Distr...
Build...

JAMESTOWN (MILL) ROAD

To Jamestown Island

N

Public Hospital
(Eastern Lunatic Asylum)

To Cedar Grove Cemetery

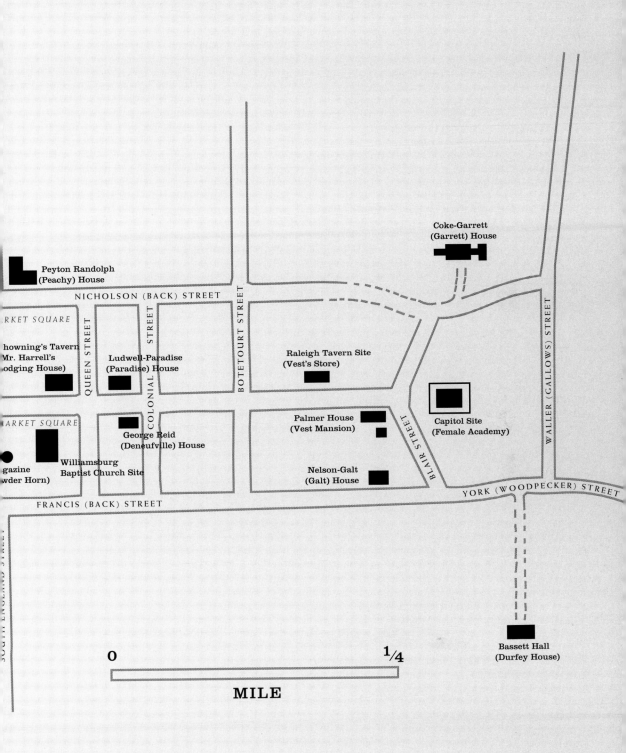

Coke-Garrett
(Garrett) House

Peyton Randolph
(Peachy) House

NICHOLSON (BACK) STREET

MARKET SQUARE

howning's Tavern
Mr. Harrell's
odging House)

Ludwell-Paradise
(Paradise) House

Raleigh Tavern Site
(Vest's Store)

QUEEN STREET

COLONIAL STREET

BOTETOURT STREET

WALLER (GALLOWS) STREET

MARKET SQUARE

George Reid
(Deneufville) House

Palmer House
(Vest Mansion)

Capitol Site
(Female Academy)

BLAIR STREET

agazine
owder Horn)

Williamsburg
Baptist Church Site

Nelson-Galt
(Galt) House

FRANCIS (BACK) STREET

YORK (WOODPECKER) STREET

SOUTH ENGLAND STREET

Bassett Hall
(Durfey House)

0   1/4

MILE

Capitol Site (Female Academy)

At the east end of Duke of Gloucester Street is located the site of the colonial Capitol. Foundations were laid in 1701 and the original structure was occupied and in use by 1704. In 1747, a fire gutted the interior, and a second Capitol building was erected and opened in 1753. The Colonial Williamsburg Foundation has reconstructed the first Capitol of 1704–1747 and placed it on the original foundation.

During the Civil War, a visitor to the city would not have seen the remains of either colonial Capitol building. The building was abandoned after the Revolution, and the eastern half was pulled down in 1793. In 1832, the remainder was destroyed by fire.

In 1849, the site of the old Capitol was given to the Williamsburg Female Academy by an act of the Virginia Assembly. A ladies' seminary had existed in Williamsburg since at least 1833, but with the donated land, a major academy was constructed.

In antebellum Virginia, academies were defined as "private schools, commonly established by a few public-spirited individuals in a county or neighborhood, who erect suitable buildings, and provide requisite teachers." Apparently the Williamsburg Female Academy was an exclusive school, as tuition was advertised in 1849 to be $165 for day students and $260 for boarding students annually.

With the secession of Virginia and the coming of war, the Female Academy was closed and the young ladies sent home. The building was not abandoned, however. It was here that Mrs. Letitia Tyler Semple, a Williamsburg resident and daughter of ex-President John Tyler, established what was to be the first Confederate military hospital in the South.

As Virginia seceded, Mrs. Semple was with her husband, James, a United States Navy paymaster stationed in New York. They immediately returned to Virginia, where her husband later served as paymaster on board the ironclad CSS *Virginia*. During their homeward journey, however, Mrs. Semple met a friend who mentioned that more soldiers died from sickness than from bullets. The friend suggested that hospitals should be established.

Upon her arrival in Richmond in May 1861, Mrs. Semple met with her father, then a member of the Confederate Congress, and the

A prewar view of the Williamsburg Female Academy, which was built on the site of the old colonial Capitol building.

Confederate secretary of war, Pope Walker. She obtained permission to establish a military hospital in Williamsburg.

The Female Academy building was selected, and tradition says that Mrs. Semple made the first bed or cot herself. Confederate General Lafayette McLaws, commanding a Georgia brigade, was impressed by the spirit of Mrs. Semple. Upon meeting her at the hospital, he stated, "I hadn't been in the room more than five minutes when, if sir, she had said to me, '[McLaws], bring me a bucket of water from the spring,' I would have done it."

Confederate surgeons were assigned to the hospital, and it began receiving patients in late May 1861. The building served this purpose until the evacuation of the city following the Battle of Williamsburg. Confederate wounded were left behind under the care of their own surgeons as the Union army entered the city. The hospital then served the wounded of both armies and later was used as a Federal barracks until the end of the war.

Coke-Garrett House (Garrett House)

At the far east end of Nicholson Street (Back Street) stands the Coke-Garrett House. The east and west sections, dating from the eighteenth century, were joined by the two-story center portion about 1836–1837. The brick office on the east end dates from around 1810.

Dr. Robert M. Garrett, a graduate of Jefferson Medical College in Philadelphia, owned the house during the war. After the Battle of Williamsburg, his house, office, and front yard became a field hospital. Though a Confederate sympathizer, Dr. Garrett was commended by both sides for giving medical attention to all wounded, regardless of the color of their uniforms.

A postwar view of the Coke-Garrett House. The front lawn served as a field hospital for both sides after the Battle of Williamsburg, May 5, 1862.

Bassett Hall (Durfey House)

Today, Bassett Hall is best remembered as the Williamsburg home of Mr. and Mrs. John D. Rockefeller, Jr., who used it during their visits to the city. Bassett Hall takes its name from Colonel Burwell Bassett, who owned the property for nearly forty years at the beginning of the nineteenth century. Colonel Goodrich Durfey purchased Bassett Hall in 1845. It was here that one of the more engaging stories of Williamsburg's Civil War period occurred.

After the Battle of Williamsburg, Captain John Willis Lea of the Fifth North Carolina Infantry was taken prisoner. Lea had resigned from the U. S. Military Academy at the war's start to fight for the Confederacy. Known as "Gimlet" to his West Point classmates, Lea had been severely wounded and was offered assistance by a Union officer. Instead, Captain Lea accepted the invitation of Mrs. Durfey to recuperate in her home on Francis Street. There he fell in love with the Durfeys' daughter Margaret, and they were married in August 1862.

Captain George Armstrong Custer of General McClellan's staff received permission from McClellan to visit his wounded classmate and became Lea's best man. Custer described the wedding in a letter to his sister:

(*Top*) A postwar view of Bassett Hall.

(*Above*) George Armstrong Custer (*right*) with a captured Confederate officer. This photograph was taken about three weeks after the Battle of Williamsburg.

41

I was at the residence of the bride long before the appointed hour. Both (the bride, and her cousin, Maggie) were dressed in white with a simple wreath of flowers upon their heads. I never saw two prettier girls. L(ea) was dressed in a bright new rebel uniform . . . trimmed with gold lace. I wore my full uniform of blue. . . . The minister soon arrived, and at nine precisely we took our places upon the floor. . . . L. made the responses in a clear and distinct tone. The bride made no response whatever except to the first question. She was evidently confused and excited, though she afterward said (laughing) that she neglected to respond purposely, so as to be free from any obligation.

On the way to supper, Custer observed to the bridesmaid that he could not see how so strong a secessionist as she could take the arm of a Union officer. She replied, "You ought to be in our army." Custer continued:

I remained with Lea, or rather, at his father-in-law's house, for two weeks, and never had so pleasant a visit among strangers, Cousin Maggie would regale me by singing and playing on the piano, "My Maryland," "Dixie," "For Southern Rights, Hurrah," etc. We were all fond of cards and would play for the Southern Confederacy. . . . When doing so Lea and I were the only players, while the ladies were spectators . . . he representing the South, I the North. Lea has since been exchanged and now is fighting for what he supposes are his rights.

After the war, John Lea became an Episcopal clergyman and served parishes in West Virginia. Custer was promoted to the rank of brigadier general at the age of twenty-three and became known as the "Boy General." He remained with the army after the war as a lieutenant colonel and was killed at Little Bighorn in 1876.

Young Captain Custer had other Williamsburg experiences. On the day before the Battle of Williamsburg, he traveled up in an observation balloon, just east of the town. It was Custer who discovered and informed his corps commander, Union General Edwin Sumner, that the Confederates were retreating toward Williamsburg. During the battle itself, he received two citations for bravery. Under the eyes of Union General Winfield Scott Hancock, Custer participated in a charge that captured a Confederate battle flag, the first taken by the new Army of the Potomac.

(*Top*) Margaret Durfey.

(*Above*) Captain John W. Lea, Fifth North Carolina Infantry.

Nelson-Galt House (Galt House)

At the corner of Francis and Blair Streets stands the Nelson-Galt House. This dwelling was once owned by Thomas Nelson of Yorktown—militia general, governor of Virginia, and signer of the Declaration of Independence. By 1861, it was the property of Dr. John Minson Galt II, the superintendent of the state-operated Eastern Lunatic Asylum. Dr. Galt did not reside in the house, however, but lived with his sister, "Sallie" Maria Galt, in the superintendent's house on the asylum grounds.

After the Union occupation and the death of her brother in May 1862, Sallie Galt was forced to leave the superintendent's house and return to the Galt family home on east Francis Street. Here she remained for the rest of the war, attended by two family slaves. From her porch, Sallie Galt experienced the war firsthand. Federal troops patrolled the street and were occasionally chased about by Confederate raiders. On one occasion, she gave out food to South Carolina cavalrymen who paused by her yard. Other families sometimes stayed with her when their homes came under fire. Twice in 1864, Sallie was pressured to take the oath of allegiance to the United States; twice she refused. It was only through the intercession of the social reformer and superintendent of Union nurses, Dorothea Dix, a friend of the Galt family, that Sallie was permitted to remain in her home. Miss Dix subsequently visited Williamsburg and was a guest of Sallie Galt at her residence.

A postwar photograph of the Nelson-Galt House.

Palmer House (Vest Mansion)

The Vest mansion, today called the Palmer House, was in 1861 nearly twice the size it is presently. Constructed in the 1750s on the site
of an earlier structure, it was originally the home of John Palmer,
lawyer and treasurer of the College of William and Mary. In 1857, the
house was enlarged by its new owner, Mr. William W. Vest, a prominent merchant of the town, whose store occupied the site of the
Raleigh Tavern after the tavern's destruction by fire in 1859. His wife
was considered peculiar because she had lost several children and had
them buried in the backyard beneath her windows. When the Union
army approached, Mr. Vest fled Williamsburg with his family.

Situated on the east end of Duke of Gloucester Street (Main
Street), the Vest house served as the headquarters for Confederate
General John Magruder and later for the Confederate commanding
general, Joseph E. Johnston. After the Battle of Williamsburg, the
house was taken over by the Union commander, General George B.
McClellan, and his staff. General McClellan stayed in Williamsburg
only a few days, during which time he played the tourist. He wrote his
wife on May 6, 1862 (the day after the Battle of Williamsburg):

> This is a beautiful town; several very old houses, pretty gardens.
> I have taken possession of a very fine old house which Joe
> Johnston occupied as headquarters. It has a lovely flower garden
> and conservatory. If you were here I should be inclined to spend
> some weeks here.

After McClellan's departure, the house was used as an office for
the Federal provost marshals, or military police, who occupied the city.
One of these was Captain (later Major) David E. Cronin of the First
New York Mounted Rifles, who made several sketches of the town and
later wrote his recollections of his wartime stay in Williamsburg.

Cronin tells us that the interior of the house was "tastefully and
richly furnished." He describes "costly carpets, cushioned easy-chairs,
cut glass chandeliers, pier and mantel mirrors." Major Cronin also left
us an account of a murder that occurred in Williamsburg in October
1863. It appears that a drunken Union sergeant named William Boyle
was picked up by the picket guard posted on York Street (Woodpecker
Street) and brought before the provost marshal, a Lieutenant W. W.

The Vest mansion. Drawn by David Cronin.

Disosway. In a rage, Boyle pulled out his pistol and shot the lieutenant on the steps of the front porch of the Vest house. Disosway's body was taken to a local undertaker to be prepared for funeral services and shipment to his home. Disosway was only nineteen years old when he was killed. Because of his youth, his remains were visited by a number of the ladies of the town, who brought flowers that were placed in the coffin.

Sergeant Boyle was arrested, court-martialed, and sentenced to death. An order of President Lincoln, however, temporarily suspended the execution of capital sentences, and Boyle was held at Fort Magruder. There, in February 1864, he escaped with the assistance of one of his guards. He made his way to Confederate lines, where he offered military information in exchange for his freedom. The guard who confessed to aiding Boyle's escape was himself court-martialed, condemned, and executed.

The Vest house served a number of Union army provost marshals throughout the occupation and was later occupied by the Freedmen's Bureau in 1865. In 1907, Lieutenant Disosway's two unmarried sisters visited Williamsburg during the Jamestown Exposition to see the site where their brother had been killed.

Raleigh Tavern Site (Vest's Store)

The Raleigh Tavern, which accommodated famous patriots and witnessed important events of the eighteenth century, was no longer standing at the beginning of the Civil War. The original structure survived until 1859, when it was destroyed by fire. The tavern was remembered as a two-story structure with front and back porches and a separate entrance for ladies and gentlemen. It stood adjacent to a store owned by William W. Vest, a city merchant. This building was also destroyed by the 1859 fire. In 1860, Vest rebuilt a larger store upon the tavern site. With the Federal advance in 1862, Vest departed the town with his family. Following the Battle of Williamsburg, his store housed wounded soldiers.

An early twentieth-century view of the Vest Store (renamed for L. W. Lane, Jr.) on the site of the Raleigh Tavern. The store served as a Confederate hospital before and after the Battle of Williamsburg.

George Reid House (Deneufville House)

This house, on the southwest corner of Duke of Gloucester and Colonial Streets, dates to the late eighteenth century. Known as the Deneufville house in 1862, it held a confectionery store. On the day of the Battle of Williamsburg, Victoria King, the seventeen-year-old refugee daughter of a Confederate surgeon, stood in front of this site all day and handed out biscuits and meat to passing Confederates.

The Southern commander, General Joseph E. Johnston, rode past and shouted to his men, "That's what we're fighting for, boys." As the last Confederates were retreating through the town, Victoria King later wrote, "An officer stopped his horse before me, and, handing me his sword, requested that I clean it and save it until he returned. I cleaned the sword—it was a very beautiful weapon—, but its owner never came back to claim it."

The George Reid House earlier in this century.

Ludwell-Paradise House (Paradise House)

D. U. BARZIZA.

Decimus et Ultimus Barziza as a member
of the Texas legislature in 1874.

The Ludwell-Paradise House on Duke of Gloucester Street was origi-
nally constructed around 1755. Restored by the Colonial Williamsburg
Foundation to its eighteenth-century appearance, it was the home of
Lucy Ludwell Paradise in the years following the Revolution. While in
Europe, Mrs. Paradise's daughter, also named Lucy, married a Venetian
count, Antonio Barziza. Their son, Philip Ignatius Barziza, came to
America to claim the house after his grandmother died at the Eastern
Lunatic Asylum in 1814. In order to retain his inheritance, he became
an American citizen and remained in Williamsburg, marrying a local
girl, Cecilia Amanda Bellette. He later became a keeper at the Lunatic
Asylum where his grandmother had died.

It was in the Paradise house that the Barziza family grew to ten
children, the last a boy christened Decimus et Ultimus Barziza. This
"tenth and last" child became known as "Dessie" to his friends and
family. He grew up in town and attended the College of William and
Mary. Graduating in 1857, he emigrated to Texas and there earned a
degree in law in 1859.

In May 1861, three months after Texas entered the Confederacy,
Dessie Barziza was commissioned a first lieutenant of his Texas county
militia company, the "Robertson Five Shooters." In August, the company was dispatched to Virginia, where it arrived after twenty-seven
days of travel by train, boat, cart, and on foot.

A postwar view of the Ludwell-Paradise House, the birthplace of Decimus et Ultimus Barziza.

Barziza's company became Company C, Fourth Texas Infantry, and was assigned to the soon-to-be famous "Texas Brigade" of General John Bell Hood. Ordered first to northern Virginia, the Texans were then sent to Yorktown in early 1862. On the afternoon of May 4, 1862, Lieutenant Decimus et Ultimus Barziza led his company up Duke of Gloucester Street (Main Street) in Williamsburg, past the very house in which he had been born.

There must not have been much opportunity to stop and visit with old friends and family, for the Confederate army was in retreat toward Richmond. Barziza's company did not participate in the Battle of Williamsburg the next day but received its baptism of fire at Eltham's Landing on the Pamunkey River on May 7. Falling back toward Richmond, Barziza was promoted to captain and served in the bloody Seven Days' Campaign around Richmond. Later, he was twice wounded and taken prisoner at Gettysburg. Sent north to prison, Captain Barziza escaped and made his way to Canada and then Bermuda. He finally reentered the Confederacy through the Union naval blockade, arriving in Wilmington, North Carolina. He returned to service with Lee's army.

After the war, Dessie Barziza returned to his adopted Texas, where he served in the state legislature. He died in Houston in 1882.

Market Square

In the center of Williamsburg is Market Square, so called because of the city markets held here since the founding of the town. Fairs, militia musters, and public gatherings took place here throughout the eighteenth century. Today the Colonial Williamsburg Foundation has restored and reconstructed several of the principal structures to their colonial appearance.

A self-portrait of Captain David Cronin of the First New York Mounted Rifles and Mr. William Peachy of Williamsburg, shown in what is now the garden of Chowning's Tavern.

On the east end of Market Square on Duke of Gloucester Street (Main Street) stands the reconstruction of Chowning's Tavern, but in 1862 this was the site of a lodging house kept by a Mr. Harrell. Later this building was added to and was known as the "Colonial Inn," serving until the 1930s. During the Union occupation it was taken over by the Federal army as a commissary, and a large United States flag was placed on the front of the building over the sidewalk. In order to avoid walking under it, the ladies of Williamsburg would detour out into the street. The soldiers obtained a larger flag and stretched it across the entire street.

Just down Duke of Gloucester Street, directly in front of the present reconstructed Magazine Guardhouse, stood a Greek Revival structure, the Williamsburg Baptist Church. Constructed in 1856, it served as a hospital for Confederate wounded during and after the Battle of Williamsburg. Victoria King, a refugee from Hampton, carried buttermilk to the wounded there and was horrified to discover a pile of amputated arms and legs in the basement. Several residents of the town told of military surgeons performing amputations here in the days immediately following the battle. Mrs. Cynthia Coleman mentioned in

The Williamsburg Baptist Church served as a Confederate hospital following the battle outside the town. Confederates who died here were temporarily buried on the green to the right.

her memoirs seeing an African-American man who had lost both his feet after he was brought in from the battlefield outside town.

The Confederates who died in this church were buried in large square pits on the west side of the building close to the basement windows. After the war, the bodies were removed to the Bruton Parish Church yard. Near the end of the war, the basement of the Baptist church was used as a school for newly freed slave children. The church was demolished in 1934, when Market Square was restored to its colonial appearance.

Standing beside the church was the eighteenth-century Magazine, or Powder Horn, as it was called then. The outer brick wall was torn down in the 1850s, and the lower floor was used as a market house before the war. The upper story had been used as a Baptist meeting-house before the construction of the adjacent church.

In 1861, the Magazine was used to store Confederate ordnance, and during the Battle of Williamsburg, the surrounding green was used as a field hospital. The Magazine itself appears to have been used to hold Confederate stragglers taken up as the Union army entered the city. With its brick wall reconstructed, the Magazine has now been restored to its late eighteenth-century appearance.

Across the street from the Magazine stood the Williamsburg and James City County Courthouse. For the first year of the war, it housed Confederate volunteers as they arrived in the city. Following the Battle of Williamsburg, the Courthouse served as a hospital and morgue. During this period, the interior woodwork was apparently torn out for use as firewood, as the building was afterwards described as being "minus doors and windows." General McClellan had issued orders

The Powder Horn.

Camp of Irv

protecting private property when he entered Williamsburg, but this mandate seems not to have applied to public buildings.

Williamsburg's city court was suspended during the Union occupation because the town was under martial law. When the city courts resumed after the war, they met in the basement of the Williamsburg Baptist Church until the Courthouse could once again be made serviceable. The building functioned as the courthouse until 1931.

The District Court Building (no longer standing) stood across the street from the Courthouse. Behind the Magazine, on Francis Street, stood the clerk's record office. It was here that the records for the city of Williamsburg and James City County were stored. With the threat of invasion in 1861, these records were removed to a warehouse in Richmond for safekeeping. In April 1865, records dating to the early seventeenth century were destroyed by fire when the Confederates evacuated Richmond.

(*Above*) A postwar photograph of the Magazine and District Court Building.

(*Opposite, top*) A wartime view of "The Powder Horn," or Magazine, on Market Square. Drawn by David Cronin.

(*Opposite, bottom*) The Williamsburg Courthouse with Federal cavalry encamped to the side, on Market Square. Drawn by David Cronin.

John Greenhow Store (City Hotel)

The site of the reconstructed John Greenhow Store on Duke of Gloucester Street was occupied before the Civil War by the City Hotel. According to a resident of the period, it was a two and one-half story house with a long front porch and a separate ladies' entrance. The basement contained a barroom. As refugees and Confederate soldiers filled Williamsburg during the war's first year, hotel accommodations in the town became scarce and spartan. A Confederate officer complained of paying one dollar for "the meanest breakfast."

In early 1862, some two hundred Louisiana troops, with the assistance of the town's residents, celebrated Mardi Gras with a procession through the streets. The carnival ended at the City Hotel, where a dinner was given for General John B. Magruder and his staff. During the festivities, members of the "Crescent Rifles" from New Orleans played a practical joke on their commander. A young New Orleans soldier was made up as a female and introduced to General Magruder. As the general entertained the young "woman" with food, drink, and conversation, several of the soldier's companions slipped upstairs into the room above. There, they ripped up a featherbed and stuffed the feathers through a hole in the ceiling. As the feathers fell onto the general, the pranksters cried, "This is a Louisiana snowstorm!"

Next to the hotel stood a barber shop that had been operated by Leroy Randolph, a free mulatto. The shop was pulled down and used for kindling wood during the war. Although General McClellan's order to respect private property was in effect, any residence or business from which the owner had fled was considered abandoned. Unfortunately, many residents felt they would be safer elsewhere, and their abandoned buildings were dismantled or torn down to provide firewood and building materials for the occupation forces.

To the west, opposite Palace green, stood a structure known as the Old Coach House. It was two stories high in the center with two sheds on either side. Before the war, it had been used as a storage area for carriages and afforded sleeping quarters for coachmen and drivers. In an attempt to stop Confederate raids, the Union occupation troops positioned a large cannon in the middle of Duke of Gloucester Street, facing the college. The Old Coach House was used as quarters by the artillerymen who manned this gun. The cannon was never known to have been fired.

Peyton Randolph House (Peachy House)

William Peachy and family about 1860.

This original eighteenth-century house, situated on the northeast corner of North England and Nicholson Streets, was once the home of Peyton Randolph, Speaker of the House of Burgesses just before the Revolution. Before the siege at Yorktown in 1781, it served as the headquarters for the French commander, the Comte de Rochambeau. In 1824, when General Lafayette returned to America, he also stayed here as a guest.

By 1861, the house was owned by William Peachy, a successful lawyer of the city. A captured Confederate cavalry officer, Major William H. Payne, recuperated here, cared for by Peachy and his family. Severely wounded during the fighting of May 5, 1862, Major Payne's injury would not heal properly, and it was feared he would die. Learning of his wound, his pregnant wife, Mary, was determined to secure his release and return him home for care.

Leaving Danville, where she had fled as a refugee, Mrs. Payne traveled to Richmond and obtained permission to cross the military lines to Williamsburg. Pass in hand, she made her way to Alexandria and Baltimore, where she boarded a steamer to Fort Monroe at Hampton. Once there, she persuaded Federal authorities to allow her to proceed to Williamsburg.

Asking directions to Mr. Peachy's house, Mary Payne found her badly wounded husband on the front porch. She personally attended him over the next few days and managed to secure his parole.

The couple returned to their home in Warrenton, Virginia, where Major Payne recovered partially from his wounds and was exchanged. He was again wounded and captured in the Gettysburg campaign, exchanged once more, and received a promotion to brigadier general in November 1864. Wounded a third time at Five Forks in April 1865, General Payne was captured on the night of President Lincoln's assassination and was finally released to return home to his wife in May 1865.

Confederate General William H. Payne. Payne was a major in the Fourth Virginia Cavalry during the Battle of Williamsburg.

Grissell Hay Lodging House
(Montague Thompson House)

On the northwest corner of Nicholson and North England Streets is the restored Grissell Hay Lodging House. During the Civil War the house was occupied by Montague Thompson and his sister, Julia Thompson Sully. Tradition tells of an amusing incident that occurred here in the later days of the war. One day, Mrs. Sully was in conversation with her neighbors across a garden. During this chatter, it was suggested that Mrs. Sully "tell Capt. Bolling that he had better be more careful. . . . If he isn't more careful, the Yankees will get him."

The next morning, Mrs. Sully found herself facing the Union provost marshal. The conversation had been overheard and reported, and she was suspected of hiding a Confederate officer in her home. Mrs. Sully quietly agreed to give him up and proceeded to lead an escort of soldiers to arrest Captain Bolling.

Guiding the guards to the backyard of her home, she pointed out her chickens and said, "There's General Lee. That other one is General Magruder. And that fellow," pointing out a large cock, "is Captain Bolling. You can have him if you can catch him!"

The Grissell Hay Lodging House in the late 1920s.

St. George Tucker House

The St. George Tucker House, located on the north side of Market Square, was originally owned by St. George Tucker, a noted jurist and veteran of George Washington's army. Tucker had the structure moved from the edge of Palace green to Market Square and reoriented to face south. His son Nathaniel Beverley Tucker, a law professor at William and Mary and a judge, inherited the house in 1838. Among other accomplishments, Nathaniel Beverley Tucker wrote a book in 1836 entitled *The Partisan Leader*, which predicted a Southern confederacy and a civil war twenty-five years before the fact.

In 1842, a young German refugee, Charles Frederic Ernest Minnegerode, arrived in Williamsburg. Minnegerode, a professor of Greek and Latin at the college, was taken in as a boarder by Judge and Mrs. Tucker. For Christmas in 1842, the young professor suggested a traditional German holiday party for the children of the house. At this celebration, the Tuckers decorated the first recorded Christmas tree in Virginia; several of the children remembered the "Christmas tree party" for the rest of their lives.

Charles Minnegerode went on to become an Episcopal clergyman in 1847 and rector of St. Paul's Church in Richmond in 1856. During the Civil War years, St. Paul's became one of the most important churches in the Confederacy. Minnegerode baptized Confederate President Jefferson Davis on May 6, 1862, and counted many other government and military leaders among his wartime parishioners. On Sunday, April 2, 1865, the Reverend Mr. Minnegerode was performing the Communion service when word was brought to President Davis that General Lee's lines were broken and Richmond was to be evacuat-

An early twentieth-century photograph of the St. George Tucker House.

A prewar portrait of Cynthia Beverley Tucker Coleman.

ed. Following the war, Minnegerode ministered to Jefferson Davis while Davis was imprisoned by Federal authorities at Fort Monroe.

By 1862, the Tucker House was occupied only by Judge Tucker's daughters and widow; his sons and son-in-law were serving with the Confederate army. One of the daughters, Cynthia Beverley Tucker Coleman, later wrote that during the battle outside town, "All day long we heard the booming of cannon and the rattle of musketry. . . . All day long the wounded were coming in."

That night the house was crowded with wet, tired, and wounded Confederate soldiers. One officer even slept under the piano. Mrs. Coleman's husband, a Confederate surgeon, stayed until dawn and departed with the rear guard.

A few hours later, Mrs. Coleman and her mother watched with apprehension as the town filled with Federal troops. Market Square was covered with horses and wagons, and Palace green was taken over by Union cavalry. Over the next two months, Mrs. Coleman protected her house and worked at surviving the occupation. She left Williamsburg in July 1862 to seek news about her brothers and husband. Although she attempted to go home several times, she was unable to return to Williamsburg through the lines until after the war.

Governor's Palace Site

Completed in 1722, the Governor's Palace served seven royal governors and the first two governors of the new Commonwealth of Virginia, Patrick Henry and Thomas Jefferson. After the government moved to Richmond in 1780, the empty Palace served as a hospital following the siege at Yorktown. In December 1781, the main building caught fire and burned to the ground. In the next few months, the remains were pulled down and the bricks sold.

By 1861, only the east and west advance buildings were still standing, both being used as residences. After the Battle of Williamsburg, one of the buildings was listed as being under repair and the other as serving as the hospital of the Third Pennsylvania Cavalry. During the Federal army occupation, these last remnants of royal government in Virginia were pulled down for their bricks.

North of these structures was a tract of land called Palace Farm. Castor beans were raised here and used in what seems to have been a prewar factory for producing castor oil. The iron cubes used for pressing the oil were sold as junk in 1865.

(*Top*) A postwar photograph showing the ruins of the Palace west advance building, destroyed by Federal troops during the town's occupation. The Saunders House can be seen to the right and the steeple of Bruton Parish Church is to the left in the distance.

(*Above*) The west advance building being used as a residence, 1859–1860.

Robert Carter House (Saunders or Page House)

In 1862, the Robert Carter House on Palace green was called the Page house but was owned by Robert Saunders, Jr., one of the wealthiest men in the city. He owned the entire plot of land now bounded by Palace green and Nassau and Henry Streets. Saunders had been the president of the College of William and Mary, a professor of mathematics, and mayor. He was highly esteemed, owned a plantation on the York River, and owned more slaves than anyone else in Williamsburg. A "colored burying ground" was located toward the rear of Saunders's Williamsburg property.

As the Confederate army retreated westward through Williamsburg, Mr. Saunders and his family abandoned their house, leaving the dinner plates on the table, and fled the city. Union soldiers ransacked the unoccupied house, stealing or destroying priceless furniture, books, and papers. Union cavalry used the building and grounds as a stable. Many historical documents, some dating to the eighteenth century, that Mrs. Saunders had inherited from her father, former Virginia Governor John Page, were lost forever. An eyewitness wrote:

> The invaders ransacked the house from cellar to roof; there was no one to ask McClellan to protect it. I have never looked upon a more deplorable picture of the ravages of war than when standing amid the litter of half destroyed books, papers and documents. . . . Shattered marble busts and statuary, fragments of ornamental book cases, heaps of old engravings, loose manuscripts, vellum bound volumes of precious colonial newspapers . . . mixed with straw and mud on every side. Hundreds of heavy-booted and spurred cavalrymen had played football with every thing of value in the house.

In the early days of the Federal occupation, the house was used as the provost marshal's office. After the war, Saunders returned to Williamsburg from Richmond, where he had been an officer in the Confederate quartermaster's corps.

A postwar view of the Robert Carter House, home of Robert Saunders in 1860.

Robert Saunders.

60

Palace Green (Confederate Monument Site)

The south end of Palace green was the original location of the Confederate monument erected by the United Daughters of the Confederacy and the citizens of Williamsburg and James City County, and dedicated on May 5, 1908. With the restoration of the city to its eighteenth-century appearance by the Colonial Williamsburg Foundation, this monument was removed in the 1930s and now stands in front of the Williamsburg–James City County Courthouse on South Henry Street. The monument reads:

1861–1865
To The
Confederate Soldiers And
Sailors Of Williamsburg
And James City County
Lord God Of Hosts, Be With Us Yet,
Lest We Forget, Lest We Forget!

The Confederate monument on Palace green.

Bruton Parish Church

The present Bruton Parish Church building has been in use since 1715, serving as the Anglican and later Episcopal Church of Williamsburg. It sits in close proximity to the site of an even earlier church constructed in 1683. In the 1750s, a pipe organ was installed in the sanctuary. Peter Pelham, harpsichordist, music teacher, and keeper of the Public Gaol, was appointed the church's first organist.

In 1861, Peter Pelham's great-grandson, John Pelham of Alabama, resigned just before graduating from the United States Military Academy and traveled to Virginia to fight for the Confederacy. On the evening of May 5, 1862, following the battle outside town, Captain Pelham led his battery of horse artillery down Duke of Gloucester Street (Main Street), past the church where his great-grandfather had worshiped and played the organ more than one hundred years earlier.

Later famous as the "Gallant Pelham," John Pelham served in more than sixty engagements and received the praise of Confederate Generals Robert E. Lee and Jeb Stuart. Promoted to major, the youthful artillerist was killed in March 1863 at Kelly's Ford, Virginia.

Following the Battle of Williamsburg, Bruton Parish Church, like all public buildings and many private homes, served as a hospital. Accounts mention that even the chancel of the church was littered with the dead and dying. Mrs. Cynthia Coleman later wrote that the day after the battle, she accompanied "Mrs. S" (Letitia Tyler Semple) to visit the wounded in the church. They were obliged to cross Palace green, which was filled with Federal cavalry, but were not bothered by the invaders. Upon reaching the church, the two ladies began comforting the wounded. There they discovered a "snivling, fawning fellow in Federal uniform." He informed the ladies that the hospital scene distressed him and that it had given him "great pain" to take up arms against "our people," as he was a "Southern man." An incensed Mrs.

(*Left*) Bruton Parish Church, 1864. Drawn by David Cronin.

(*Right*) John Pelham.

Semple compared him to "Cain who killed his brother Abel." Mrs. Coleman remembered, "He slunk away and we did not see him again."

After the wounded had been removed, the church resumed serving the parish. In February 1863, services were suspended by the Federal provost marshal in response to disloyal statements made by the rector, Thomas M. Ambler, in his sermons. Mr. Ambler also apparently refused to include the prayer for the president of the United States.

The Bruton Communion silver was carried away for safety during the war by a slave; it was later returned to the church.

At least forty Confederate soldiers, most killed during the Battle of Williamsburg, are buried in the churchyard. Additionally, several Confederates who died in the Williamsburg Baptist Church were eventually interred here. Most lie in unknown graves, but there is a monument, erected in 1887, listing the names of twenty-nine men from Alabama, Florida, Mississippi, North Carolina, Louisiana, South Carolina, and Virginia.

Among the marked graves is that of Colonel George T. Ward of the Second Florida Infantry. Mrs. Coleman remembered:

> A Florida Regiment was sent back from above to the Battle field, as they passed a house in the Town to which the wounded had been carried, a girl young and fair, waved before them a blood-stained cloth, calling out "go and avenge this blood." . . . they did avenge it, but with terrible loss to themselves, for their gallant colonel while shouting his battle-cry in defense of the women of Williamsburg was shot and fell dead from his horse. . . . I have often wondered if Col. Ward had no family or friends in his own State to honour his remains by removal to his native soil.

Another monument stands to James Semple, who served aboard the ironclad CSS *Virginia*, and his wife, who accompanied Mrs. Coleman on her visit to the church when it was a hospital.

Inside the north transept is a tablet that reads:

IN MEMORY OF
THE
CONFEDERATE
SOLDIERS
who fell in the
BATTLE OF WILLIAMSBURG
May the 5th 1862
And those, who died of
the wounds received in
the same.
THEY DIED FOR US.

Bowden-Armistead House (Bowden House)

In Virginia in 1861, difficult decisions had to be made about whether to remain loyal to the "Grand Old Union" or to secede with one's native state. Some Virginians chose to speak out against secession and the Confederate government. Several hundred of these dissenters were confined in prison in Richmond, charged with "suspected political infidelity." Though few Williamsburg residents are known to have been arrested for this crime, the town had its Unionists. One of them was Lemuel J. Bowden.

Bowden was a lawyer and president of the board of overseers of the Eastern Lunatic Asylum. His house was built for him on the northeast corner of Nassau and Duke of Gloucester Streets. Completed in 1858, the house was constructed of Baltimore brick and surrounded by an iron fence purchased in Richmond. Today the Bowden-Armistead House is privately owned and is the only example of a Civil War-era brick Greek Revival house still standing in the city.

Bowden left Williamsburg in 1861 to enter the Union lines. Upon their occupation of the city, the Federal military governor installed Lem Bowden as mayor. Not all Williamsburg residents welcomed his return. Miss Harriette Cary wrote in her diary on May 12, 1862, "Bowden the Traitor is mayor of our Town." Two days later, she commented, "The Band Serenaded Mayor Bowden to-night—loud cheering heard in conclusion. Down with the Traitor! If we ever recover our power—." Even Bowden's mother considered him a traitor. An ardent secessionist, Mrs. Mildred Bowden refused to live with him and moved into a smaller house at the rear of his garden.

Lemuel Bowden later left Williamsburg to attend the Wheeling Convention, which claimed to represent the loyal Union government of Virginia. There he was elected to serve as a United States senator from Virginia. He served for less than a year, however, before he died of smallpox in Washington, D. C., at the age of forty-eight. Bowden was buried in the Congressional Cemetery.

The Bowden-Armistead House, home of
Lemuel Bowden, one of Williamsburg's
few Unionists. Bowden left here in
1861 and returned the next year to serve
briefly as mayor during the Federal
occupation of the city.

John Blair House (John T. James House)

A postwar view of the John Blair House.

Toward the western end of Duke of Gloucester Street stands the home of John Blair, Sr., nephew of the Reverend James Blair, founder and first president of the College of William and Mary. Part of the house was constructed in the early eighteenth century, making the John Blair House one of the oldest residences in Williamsburg.

Before the Civil War, it was divided into a two-family home. A baker had lived in the western half, and the Federal troops, discovering a brick oven on the property, used it for their own needs. The oven was enlarged and extended from the basement out into the backyard. Union army bakers daily made up loaves of bread that were delivered by wagon to Fort Magruder, east of the city.

African Baptist Church Site

Near the northwest corner of Francis and Nassau Streets stood the African Baptist Church, erected by the town's African-Americans. Constructed about 1855 on the site of a carriage house, it was taken over as a Confederate hospital in 1861. Sallie Galt, who lived nearby with her brother Dr. John Minson Galt II in the superintendent's house at the Lunatic Asylum, considered herself the "patron saint" of this temporary hospital. With the Union occupation, the church was returned to its congregation, which numbered 736 members by 1866. The congregation relocated in 1956, and the property was purchased by the Colonial Williamsburg Foundation. A plaque marks the site of the church.

The African Baptist Church was used as a Confederate hospital during the first year of the war.

Public Hospital (Eastern Lunatic Asylum)

The reconstructed Public Hospital as it looks now bears little resemblance to the hospital's sprawling appearance in 1861. Opened in 1773, the Public Hospital was the first public institution in British America to care for the mentally ill. Almost ninety years later, the hospital was called the Eastern Lunatic Asylum, the original building had added a third floor, and the institution had expanded to six other buildings. By 1861, there were nearly three hundred patients.

Early on the morning of May 5, 1862, citizens of the town climbed to the cupola of the hospital to observe the Battle of Williamsburg as it was fought in the distance. After Federal forces entered the town, the hospital's superintendent, Dr. John Minson Galt II, was refused entry to his beloved institution. Dr. Galt had been superintendent for twenty-one years. During that time he had labored mightily to improve the hospital and the lot of his patients. The loss of his responsibilities proved to be too much; twelve days after the Union army occupied the city, Galt died at the age of forty-three.

A prewar engraving of the Lunatic Asylum.

His obituary, written by his sister Sallie, stated:

IN MEMORIAM

Died, in Williamsburg, Va. May 18, 1862, after an illness of four days, of an affection of the stomach, to which he had been subject for many years, John M. Galt, M.D., son of the late Dr. Alexander D. Galt.

Some quietly suggested that Dr. Galt had been so taken with grief over his lost position that he had overdosed on laudanum, which he used to calm his stomach "affection."

Apparently the Federal government did not take full responsibility for the hospital's patients until March 1864. Before that time, Union officials merely provided rations to the patients and stewards as needed. In 1863, after Confederate raiders had taken U.S. government rations from the hospital, the military governor of the city threatened to send all of the patients to Richmond to be cared for by state authorities if the raids continued. The raids ended. After the war, the hospital returned to the control of a board of directors. The original building was destroyed by fire in 1885. It was reconstructed to its eighteenth-century appearance by the Colonial Williamsburg Foundation in 1985.

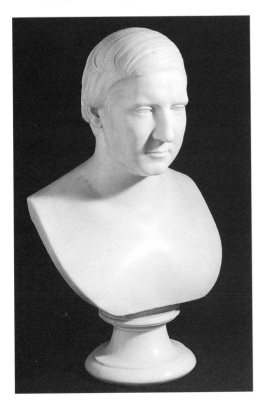

John Minson Galt II.

Cedar Grove Cemetery

On November 15, 1859, the mayor, aldermen, and Common Council of Williamsburg purchased four acres of land on South Henry Street for the sum of $400. The land was enclosed by a brick wall and became Cedar Grove, or the "new" cemetery.

After the Battle of Williamsburg, the question arose of where to bury those who had been killed in the battle or had died of their wounds. More than 250 Confederates were interred in a common grave located in the northeast section of the cemetery. Today a monument, dedicated on May 5, 1935, marks their resting place. The Union dead from the battle were buried in the National Cemetery at Yorktown.

Mrs. Cynthia Beverley Tucker Coleman, wife of a Confederate surgeon, remembered later that Confederate burials were always accompanied by women and children of the town. On one occasion, she remarked that the accompanying mourners could distinctly hear the artillery fire from the Battle of Malvern Hill, forty miles away.

The monument in Cedar Grove Cemetery marks the grave of more than 250 Confederate soldiers.

Williamsburg Theatre (Ware House Site)

One incident illustrates the sadness of what happened, not only to Williamsburg but to our nation, during the tragic time of the Civil War. John S. Charles, who was about ten years old when the Union army entered the town, recalled that after the Battle of Williamsburg, a wounded young Confederate soldier was brought into the town and taken into the private residence of Mrs. Elizabeth Ware. The Ware house stood on Duke of Gloucester Street (Main Street) on the ground presently occupied by the Williamsburg Theatre in Merchants Square. The one and one-half story frame residence had a deep cellar and a large shed on the back.

The young Confederate died soon after he was taken to the Ware house. Mrs. Ware and her married daughter placed his body in the parlor. Presently, Federal troops made the rounds of the city asking about sick or wounded soldiers. When informed of the dead Confederate, a Union soldier entered Mrs. Ware's parlor and uncovered the face of the corpse. As the women watched, it was discovered that the Union soldier was the brother of the dead Rebel.

The soldier knelt and kissed his dead brother, "thus grimly demonstrating the truth of the expression so often heard, that this War was one of 'Father against son, Brother against Brother.'"

Binns Fashion Shop (Lively House Site)

In 1861, Edward H. Lively lived in a house on the western end of town near the College of William and Mary. The house was owned by his mother and was located at the site of the present Binns Fashion Shop on Merchants Square. Here in the late 1850s Lively edited and published the local newspaper, the *Weekly Gazette and Eastern Virginia Advertiser*. He was assisted by his brother, Robert, who served as printer. The presses were apparently in the basement of the house. Lively's paper favored the formation of a militia company following John Brown's raid on the Federal arsenal at Harpers Ferry in October 1859 and supported John Breckinridge for the presidency in the election of 1860. On May 23, 1861, the Lively house was the site of the first Southern secessionist flag to be raised over the city. Edward and Robert Lively subsequently joined the Williamsburg Junior Guard, later Company C, Thirty-second Virginia Infantry.

When Federal Troops occupied Williamsburg in May 1862, the Fifth Pennsylvania Cavalry confiscated the Livelys' presses and used them to print a Union soldier's paper entitled the *Cavalier*. According to accounts at the time, Mrs. Lively vainly attempted to defend her sons' property, refusing to hand over the keys to the basement. In December 1862, the presses were relocated to Yorktown and later to Fort Monroe. After the war the Lively brothers returned to Williamsburg and reclaimed their presses. The paper began again and continues to this day as the *Virginia Gazette*, tracing a tangled ancestry to 1736.

College of William and Mary

Chartered in 1693, the College of William and Mary is the second oldest college in America. The main building, known today as the Wren Building, was originally completed in 1700 and is the oldest academic structure still in use in English-speaking America. On its south side stands the Brafferton, originally constructed in 1723 to house Indian students. To its north is located the President's House, built in 1732–1733. Today these three buildings have been restored to show their appearance from the eighteenth century until 1859, when they composed the entire college.

In 1859, a disastrous fire occurred, gutting the Wren Building. A library of eight thousand books, several antique scientific instruments, and even marble tablets on the Chapel walls were destroyed. As a result, the commencement exercises of 1859 were held in the Williamsburg Baptist Church on Market Square. Thanks to generous donations, however, the building was repaired and two Italianate towers were constructed flanking the entrance, drastically altering its appearance. The Wren Building was ready for students again by October 1859, only eight months after the fire.

On May 10, 1861, the war came to the college as the faculty suspended classes and even the president of the college, fifty-one-year-old Benjamin Stoddert Ewell, volunteered to defend the state. A West

An engraving of the Wren Building as it appeared from 1860 to 1862.

Point graduate, Ewell was the brother of Confederate General Richard Ewell. "Old Buck," as he was called, was commissioned a colonel in the Thirty-second Virginia Infantry and later served on the staff of General Joseph E. Johnston.

The college supported the Southern cause in other ways. College funds were invested in Confederate bonds to assist further in the state's defense. The Wren Building was taken over and used as a barracks as more Confederates appeared. The first volunteers to arrive were quartered in the college library, where they used the books for pillows. Eventually the building held a growing number of sick soldiers, the overflow from the military hospital at the Female Academy.

The day before the Battle of Williamsburg, General George Pickett, later of Gettysburg fame, held his brigade of Virginians in the area behind the Wren Building. The morning of the battle, the grounds were occupied by the brigade of General Jubal Early, which was being held in reserve. The Twenty-second and Thirty-eighth Virginia Regiments and the Fifth and Twenty-third North Carolina Regiments stacked arms here and tried to find cover from the rain. Later in the day, they marched through the town and into the battle, where they lost 508 men. During the battle itself, General James Longstreet, commander of the Confederate rear guard, had his headquarters here.

Throughout the rainy night following the bloodshed, the college witnessed the retreat as the Confederate troops marched through the mud past College Corner and up Richmond Road (Stage Road) toward Richmond. A white picket fence enclosing the college was quickly dismantled for firewood during the retreat.

The college buildings and grounds quickly became a field hospital. A French observer with the Union army, François d'Orléans, Prince de Joinville, observed upon entering the city that "the wounded were lying upon the very steps of the college porticoes."

After the Federal occupation, the main building became a Union barracks and commissary supply depot. Union officers occupied the Brafferton, and the President's House was inhabited by Mrs. Virginia Southall and her family. They had been offered the residence by Colonel Ewell before his departure. After Appomattox and the end of the war, the President's House was used as headquarters for the Federal troops left in Williamsburg to oversee Reconstruction.

Just beyond the college, on Stage Road, picket posts were established, and Williamsburg became the fringe of the United States military occupation. From 1862 until Grant's advance on Richmond in 1864, Williamsburg and the college were on the unofficial border between the Confederacy and the Union.

On September 9, 1862, a band of Confederate cavalry under General Henry Wise rode into Williamsburg and actually recaptured the town; they drove in the Union pickets, swept up the reserve guard, and captured the Union provost marshal, Colonel David Campbell,

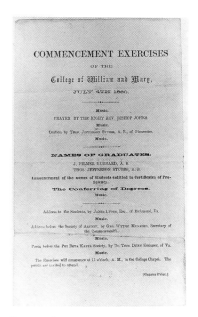

Program for the 1860 commencement ceremony at the College of William and Mary. There were only two graduates that year.

Wise's Last Raid

A Confederate raid on the Federal picket post at the College of William and Mary in 1863. The ruins of the Wren Building, burned earlier by Federal cavalry, stand in the background. The ninety-year-old statue of royal governor Botetourt survived the skirmish. Drawn by David Cronin.

asleep in his bed. The Confederates held the town briefly before being forced to withdraw. In retaliation, late in the afternoon of the same day, members of the Fifth Pennsylvania Cavalry set fire to the main building of the college. Witnesses stated that the soldiers were drunk and that they surrounded the burning building with drawn swords to prevent citizens from putting out the fire.

The empty, burned-out building was boarded up, and the 1773 statue of royal governor Lord Botetourt, which had escaped damage, was moved to the asylum for safekeeping in late 1864. There were further Confederate raids throughout the war. For protection against these attacks, the Union soldiers constructed defensive works. The windows and doors of the college opening to the north and west were bricked up, with loopholes in them for small arms. Deep ditches that extended across both Richmond (Stage) Road and Jamestown (Mill) Road were dug on the northeast and southern corners of the college. Logs ten feet long were placed into the ground and fitted with loopholes to guard against raids down the two roads. Abatis, made from the tops of oak and beech trees with limbs sharpened, were set into the ground along with chevaux-de-frise, and all were entangled with wire.

Such was the appearance of the college as the war ended. It would not be rebuilt until 1869 and would take even longer to recover financially from its Confederate investments. A memorial tablet was erected at the Wren Building by the Board of Visitors and the alumni of the college in 1914. Its inscription reads:

C.S.A.

To the memory of the professors and students who left the College of William and Mary in May 1861 and in patriotic devotion fought in defense of the Confederate States of America.

The names of seven faculty members and sixty-one students are listed.

Jamestown and Richmond Roads
(Market Line)

During the Federal occupation, a market was established outside of town to the west on Jamestown and Richmond Roads (Mill and Stage Roads). On agreed-upon days, once or twice a week, farmers from the Confederate-controlled areas outside the city could bring in their poultry and produce and sell them to the citizens of Williamsburg. The intent was to relieve the food shortages and sufferings of the town's inhabitants. Because of the amount of information and contraband that seemed to pass between buyers and sellers, the enterprise was managed by the Federal provost marshal and his men. The procedure was for the farmers and market women to gather and await the arrival of the provost guard. The sergeant of the guard would then allow the vendors to bring their wagons and goods to the market line, a set of parallel wires that separated dealers from customers. The guards stood between the wires. Despite these precautions, Captain (later Major) David Cronin of the First New York Mounted Rifles remarked that the guards "were sometimes easily flattered, by the shrewdly designing opposite sex."

Information flowed freely through the lines. Newspapers and mail were concealed in jars of butter and jam, melons, and dressed poultry. A great deal of diplomatic correspondence passed through Williamsburg in this manner, for mail coming out of the Confederacy could be remailed at the United States Post Office at Yorktown for delivery around the world. In the opposite direction, badly needed medicines, military information, and other supplies found their way into the Confederacy through this route. In 1863, the wives of two Williamsburg merchants, the Hoffhiemer brothers, were taken up by Federal picket guards for attempting to smuggle scarce items through the lines to Richmond. Upon examination, it was discovered that they had concealed boots, shoes, and bags of coffee, tea, and sugar under their hoopskirts.

On February 9, 1864, 109 Union officers being held as prisoners of war at Libby Prison in Richmond crawled through a sixty-foot tunnel and escaped. Almost half were quickly rounded up by the Confederates during the following few days. Those who managed to evade their pursuers did so by way of Williamsburg, and it was here on the Market Line that they reached the Federal forces and freedom.

Having escaped from Libby Prison, Union prisoners of war enter Federal lines at Williamsburg in 1864. Drawn by David Cronin.

Frog Pond Tavern

Just west of the modern intersection of Jamestown and Richmond Roads (Mill and Stage Roads, respectively), heading toward Richmond and across from the College of William and Mary, stood Frog Pond Tavern. Nothing remains today to mark the spot of a once-thriving establishment where legend says French officers stayed after the siege at Yorktown in 1781.

Frog Pond Tavern earned its name from a large mudhole in Stage Road that never seemed to be filled or drained. This "pond" "produced fine crops of frogs" that were gathered as a delicacy for the guests.

In 1862, the tavern was kept by a "kind-hearted and genial old fellow" called "Old By Jucks." When the Union army entered Williamsburg in May 1862, "Old By Jucks" became "highly excited and greatly alarmed." He hung a large white flag from the front of his tavern and waited for the invaders. To the advance guard of Union cavalry belonging to General George Stoneman, he presented himself with his hat in his hand. Bowing politely, he exclaimed, "Good morning Gentlemen—Come in, and have some hot biscuits and coffee."

Federal cavalry pickets on Richmond Road. Drawn by David Cronin.

Ewell Hall

Colonel Benjamin S. Ewell as a civilian after the war.

Four miles west of the College of William and Mary along Richmond Road stands Ewell Hall, the house of Benjamin Ewell, the president of the college who resigned in 1861 to enter the Confederate service. His farm, which surrounded the house, is now the site of a modern cemetery and hidden from view by outlet malls and shopping centers.

During the Confederate retreat from Williamsburg in May 1862, Colonel Ewell buried a supply of wine in his front yard. Returning after the war in 1865, he recovered his hidden cache. General McClellan briefly paused his headquarters here on May 10, 1862.

Jamestown Island

About five miles southwest of Williamsburg lies Jamestown Island, where the first permanent English colony in North America was established in 1607. From that time until 1699, Jamestown served as the capital and social center of the colony of Virginia. When the capital was moved to Williamsburg, the island fell into decay and remained the home of only a few families.

By 1861, the island belonged to Mr. William Allen of Surry County. With secession, Mr. Allen took it upon himself to begin planning defensive works there. The island's importance was not overlooked by the authorities in Richmond, however. Artillery situated on the island could command passage both up and down the James River, thus protecting Richmond. With this in mind, General Robert E. Lee, commander of the state forces, journeyed to Jamestown Island to assist in planning the sighting of gun batteries and redoubts. Eventually, using slave labor and the available military garrison, two major earthen forts and three smaller batteries were constructed.

The fortifications were never fully armed and manned, and with the evacuation of Williamsburg in 1862, the island was abandoned by the Confederates. One interesting note is that during the Confederate occupation, the armor plates manufactured in Richmond to be used by the ironclad CSS *Virginia* were tested on the island.

With the Confederate departure, the island became a refuge for contraband slaves. Later, a Union observation and picket post were established here to give warning of the passage of Southern vessels and to prevent smugglers or spies from crossing the river. After mid-1864, a telegraph line was established from the original brick church tower to Fort Magruder in Williamsburg.

Today, most of Jamestown Island belongs to the National Park Service. Some twenty acres containing the early town site belong to the Association for the Preservation of Virginia Antiquities. Although the emphasis of the site is on the seventeenth-century settlement, there are still the remains of one of the batteries and the two forts.

(*Opposite, top*) The "neglected graveyard of the first settlers" at Jamestown Island. Drawn by David Cronin.

(*Opposite, bottom*) Ruins of the church at Jamestown Island, being used as a Federal signal station, in 1864. Drawn by David Cronin.

for Confeder-

s - Doubts con-

ts - A picket

The 1860 Census of Williamsburg

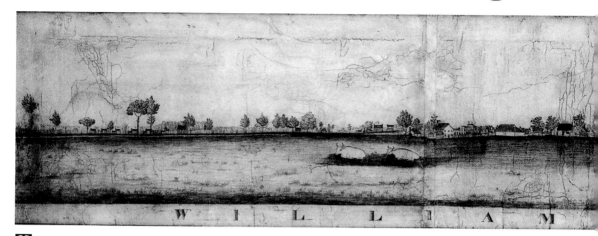

The 1860 United States Census of Williamsburg was compiled between June 18 and July 16, 1860. It enumerated 742 whites and 121 blacks on the free schedule and 743 blacks on the slave schedule. In addition, there were 270 whites and 19 blacks listed as residing at the Eastern Lunatic Asylum of the State of Virginia.

The five most prosperous citizens each held property and possessed personal estates worth more than $100,000. They were:

Name	Total Value of Property & Estate	Occupation
R. P. Waller	$253,000	Farmer
Henley Jones	$128,000	Farmer
Lucy A. Tucker	$125,000	Head of Household
William Vest	$124,350	Merchant
Robert Saunders	$108,000	Farmer

There were 288 persons recorded with an occupation on the free schedule. They were listed as:

Occupation	White Male	White Female	Black or Mulatto Male	Black or Mulatto Female	Occupation	White Male	White Female	Black or Mulatto Male	Black or Mulatto Female
Agent for Soap	1				City Sergeant	1			
Asylum Officer	6	5			Clerk	7			
Barber			1		Clerk of Court	2			
Blacksmith	2		1		Coachmaker	6			
Brickmason	2				Confectioner		1		
Capt. U.S.N.	1				Dentist	1			
Carpenter	5		1		Ditcher				3

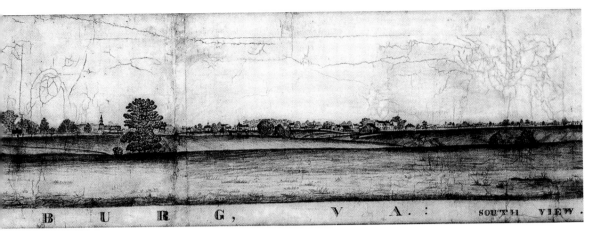

Williamsburg in 1860.

Occupation	White Male	Female	Black or Mulatto Male	Female
Dressmaker		2		
Editor	1			
Engineer	1			
Farmer	19			
Fisherman			1	
Gardener			1	
Grocer	1			
Harness Maker	3			
Hospital Matron		1		
Hospital Steward	1			
Hotel Keeper	1			
Laborer/Farm Hand	3		3	
Lawyer	10			
Mail Carrier	1			
Mantuamaker		5		
Manufacturer	1			
Mechanic	26			
Merchant	17	1		
Milliner		1		
Minister	4			
Music Professor	1			
Oysterman			2	
Painter	2			
Physician	9			
Plasterer	2			
Police Officer	1			
Postmaster	1			
Prescriptionist	1			
Printer	1			
Professor	2			
Public Officer	2			
Revenue Commissioner	1			
Seamstress		13		6
Servant	1		8	15
Shoemaker	7		2	
Shopkeeper	1			
Statuary	1			
Steamboat Fireman			1	
Superintendent	1			
Tailor/Tailoress	5	3		
Tanner	1			
Teacher	4	4		
Undertaker	1			
Washerwoman				29
Waterman	5		2	
Wheelwright			1	
Woodcutter			2	

Civil War Engagements in the Williamsburg Area, 1862–1865

Cavalry Skirmish East of Williamsburg, May 4, 1862: A prelude to the Battle of Williamsburg.

Battle of Williamsburg, May 5, 1862: A major engagement, although inconclusive. The Confederate army, retreating from Yorktown, intended to pass through Williamsburg. The Confederate rear guard, however, turned and held the Union army all day, then continued its retreat. Casualties: Union—468 killed, 1442 wounded, 347 missing. Confederate—288 killed, 975 wounded, 297 missing.

Confederate Raid on Williamsburg, September 9, 1862: Confederate cavalry occupied the city for a few hours, which led to Union retaliation and the burning of the College of William and Mary.

Skirmish at Toano (Burnt Ordinary), January 19, 1863: A Union reconnaissance up Richmond Road (Stage Road) to Burnt Ordinary.

Skirmish at Olive Branch Church, February 5, 1863: A Union reconnaissance up Richmond Road (Stage Road) to modern-day Norge, Virginia. Confederate pickets were scattered and a Virginia flag was captured. Note: The Olive Branch Church survived and is active today.

Skirmish at Six Mile Ordinary, February 7, 1863: A Union reconnaissance up Richmond Road (Stage Road). The Federal troops were ambushed and forced to return to Williamsburg.

Confederate Attempt to Capture Fort Magruder, March 29, 1863: Confederate infantry briefly occupied Williamsburg, and there was fighting on Duke of Gloucester Street (Main Street) near the College of William and Mary. The town was shelled by Federal artillery, and the Confederates withdrew.

Confederate Attempt to Capture Fort Magruder, April 11, 1863: The last serious Confederate raid on Williamsburg, this was a large attack by Confederate infantry, cavalry, and artillery. The town was shelled, and the Confederates withdrew after removing the provisions given to

The Comte de Paris riding into Yorktown to report on the Battle of Williamsburg. Drawn by Alfred Waud.

the Eastern Lunatic Asylum. After this raid, the Federal military governor threatened to send the three hundred patients from the asylum to Richmond to be cared for if the raids continued. In consequence, there were no further significant attempts to retake Williamsburg.

Union Expedition from Williamsburg, August 26, 1863: Four-day Union reconnaissance to Bottom's Bridge.

Union Expedition from Williamsburg, November 9, 1863: Union cavalry reconnaissance to New Kent Courthouse.

Union Expedition from Williamsburg, December 12, 1863: Union reconnaissance to Charles City Courthouse.

Skirmish at Toano (Burnt Ordinary), April 27, 1864: Union reconnaissance up Richmond Road (Stage Road).

Skirmish on Jamestown Road (Mill Road), Williamsburg, February 11, 1865: Confederate guerrillas attacked Union pickets west of the city.

The Armies of the Battle of Williamsburg

Includes preliminary cavalry skirmish of May 4,1862

Confederate

Commander: Joseph E. Johnston

Field Commander: James Longstreet

Second Division: Longstreet

First Brigade: Ambrose P. Hill

    1st Virginia

    7th Virginia

    11th Virginia

    17th Virginia

Second Brigade: Richard H. Anderson

    4th South Carolina (battalion)

    5th South Carolina

    6th South Carolina

    Palmetto Sharpshooters

    Louisiana Foot Rifles

    Fauquier Artillery

    Williamsburg Artillery (2 guns)

    Richmond Howitzers (2 guns)

Third Brigade: George E. Pickett

    8th Virginia

    18th Virginia

    19th Virginia

    28th Virginia

    Dearing's Virginia Battery

Fourth Brigade: Cadmus M. Wilcox

    9th Alabama

    10th Alabama

    19th Mississippi

Fifth Brigade: Roger A. Pryor

    8th Alabama

    14th Alabama

    14th Louisiana

    32nd Virginia (detachment)

    Richmond Fayette Artillery

Colston's Brigade: Raleigh E. Colston

    3rd Virginia

    13th North Carolina

    14th North Carolina

    Donaldsonville (La.) Battery (3 guns)

Fourth Division: Daniel H. Hill

Early's Brigade: Jubal A. Early

    24th Virginia

    38th Virginia

    5th North Carolina

    23rd North Carolina

Unattached:

    2nd Florida

    2nd Mississippi (battalion)

Cavalry Division: James E. B. Stuart

    3rd Virginia Cavalry

    4th Virginia Cavalry

    Wise Legion

    Jeff Davis Legion

    Stuart Horse Artillery

Union

Commander: George B. McClellan

Field Commander: Edwin V. Sumner

III Corps: Samuel P. Heintzelman

Second Division: Joseph Hooker

First Brigade: Cuvier Grover

    1st Massachusetts

    11th Massachusetts

    2nd New Hampshire

    26th Pennsylvania

Second Brigade: Nelson Taylor

    70th New York

    72nd New York

    73rd New York

    74th New York

Third Brigade: Francis E. Patterson

    5th New Jersey

    6th New Jersey

    7th New Jersey

    8th New Jersey

Confederate artillery in Fort Magruder.
Drawn by David Cronin.

Artillery: Charles S. Wainwright
    1st New York (D Battery)
    4th New York
    6th New York
    1st U.S.

Third Division: Philip Kearny
First Brigade: Charles Jameson
    57th Pennsylvania
    63rd Pennsylvania
    105th Pennsylvania
    87th New York
Second Brigade: David B. Birney
    38th New York
    40th New York
Third Brigade: Hiram G. Berry
    2nd Michigan
    5th Michigan
    37th New York

IV Corps: Erasmus D. Keyes
First Division: Darius N. Couch
Second Brigade: John Peck
    93rd Pennsylvania
    98th Pennsylvania
    102nd Pennsylvania
    55th New York
    62nd New York

Second Division: William F. Smith
First and Third Brigade: Winfield Scott Hancock
    5th Wisconsin
    49th Pennsylvania
    6th Maine
    7th Maine
    33rd New York

Cavalry Division: George Stoneman
Brigade: Philip St. George Cooke
Brigade: William H. Emory
    8th Illinois Cavalry
    McClellan Dragoons
    3rd Pennsylvania Cavalry
    1st U.S. Cavalry
    6th U.S. Cavalry
Artillery: William Hays
    2nd U.S. (B, L, M Batteries)
    3rd U.S. (C, K Batteries)

Appendix D
Williamsburg Hospitals

Williamsburg immediately after the Battle of Williamsburg. The "Brick Seminary [Female Academy on the site of the old Capitol] used as a hospital for union wounded" is above the wagons on the left.

Public buildings and homes known to have been used as hospitals before and after the Battle of Williamsburg, May 5, 1862:

Confederate Military Hospital (Female Academy at Capitol site)
Williamsburg Baptist Church (Market Square)
Courthouse and Market Square
Williamsburg Methodist Church
Bruton Parish Church
Eastern Lunatic Asylum (Public Hospital)
African Baptist Church
College of William and Mary (Wren Building) and yard
Garrett House (Coke-Garrett House)
Durfey House (Bassett Hall)
Vest's Store (Raleigh Tavern Site)
Peachy House (Peyton Randolph House)
Tucker House (St. George Tucker House)
Asylum Superintendent's House (Travis House)
Mrs. Sidney Smith's

John T. James House (John Blair House)
Mr. Darden's
Mr. Hansford's
Mr. Ambler's (Bruton Rector)
Mrs. Ware's (Williamsburg Theatre site)
Mr. Joyner's
Mr. Claibourne's
Mr. C. Waller's
Mrs. King's
Mrs. Henley Jones's
Mrs. Southall's
Mr. Maupin's
Mr. Blain's
Mr. Baylor's
Mrs. Henley's
Mr. Munford's (Tazewell Hall)
Miss Morrison's

Appendix E
Union Military Goverment in Williamsburg, 1862–1865

The Battle of Williamsburg. Drawn by David Cronin.

Colonel David Campbell
Fifth Pennsylvania Cavalry
Acting military governor, May 12–September 9, 1862. Captured by the enemy September 9, 1862.

Captain T. Hennessey
Company G, Fifth Pennsylvania Cavalry
Provost marshal, May–September 1862.

Major Christopher Kleinz
Fifth Pennsylvania Cavalry
Acting military governor and provost marshal, September 1862–August 1863. Rejoined unit August 1863.

Colonel Robert K. West
First Pennsylvania Artillery
Military governor, 1863–1864.

Sergeant John F. Fisher
Fifth Pennsylvania Cavalry
Provost marshal, August–October 6, 1863. Deserted to the enemy November 5, 1863.

Lieutenant W. W. Disosway
First New York Mounted Rifles
Provost marshal, October 7–14, 1863. Murdered October 14, 1863.

Major James Wheelan
First New York Mounted Rifles
Provost marshal, October 1863–May 1864.

Colonel W. H. P. Steere
Fourth Rhode Island Infantry
Commander, Fort Magruder, summer 1864.

Lieutenant James Matthews
Sixteenth New York Heavy Artillery
Provost marshal, May 1864.

Captain David E. Cronin
First New York Mounted Rifles
Provost marshal, May–September 1864.

Colonel J. J. Morrison
Sixteenth New York Heavy Artillery
Commander, Fort Magruder, July 1864.

Captain A. M. C. Smith
Sixteenth New York Heavy Artillery
Provost marshal, autumn 1864–1865.

Captain Henry A. Vezin
Fifth Pennsylvania Cavalry
Provost marshal, 1865.

Mr. _____ Whipple
Freedmen's Bureau
1865.

Appendix F
Williamsburg Junior Guard
Company C
Thirty-second Virginia Infantry

In 1859, in response to John Brown's raid on Harpers Ferry, the students and faculty of the College of William and Mary, along with several prominent citizens of the city, formed a militia company and elected lawyer Robert H. Armistead their captain. On paper, the men of Williamsburg were the old Sixty-eighth Regiment of the state militia, but in practice, that unit had been inactive for years. The new company was christened the "Williamsburg Junior Guard" and began to drill on the college grounds.

On April 17, 1861, Virginia passed an ordinance of secession. College President Benjamin Ewell was commissioned as a major in the Army of the State of Virginia. Ordered to gather volunteers from the surrounding area, Ewell enlisted the Williamsburg company into state service on April 28, for a term of one year.

Despite confusion, recruiting problems, and insufficient arms and equipment, other local volunteer units began gathering at Camp Page near Williamsburg. On July 1, 1861, the Thirty-second Virginia Infantry was formed from ten Peninsula companies. The new regiment numbered 670 men when it was placed into the service of the Confederate Government. Additionally, at least 20 slaves and free blacks would accompany the unit as cooks throughout the coming war. The Williamsburg Junior Guard became Company C of the Thirty-second Virginia Infantry, and Major Ewell was promoted to colonel of the regiment. Captain John A. Henley, clerk of the Circuit Court, commanded the Williamsburg company at this time.

By July 1861, when the company was issued uniforms from the Confederate Quartermaster's Department, the Junior Guard mustered ninety-three men. There were four officers and eight noncommissioned officers. In Company C's ranks were the men of the city. Their occupations were listed as students, merchants, farmers, mechanics, carpenters, lawyers, clerks, painters, shoemakers, and a host of other vocations. Their average age was 24.9.

Initially assigned to the Williamsburg line, the Thirty-second Virginia was reorganized late in 1861, losing four companies and receiving a previously detached one back in return. By January 1, 1862, the regiment could muster only 453 officers and men for duty, rather than the 1,000 called for by regulations. For the remainder of the war, the regiment consisted of seven companies instead of the normal ten.

George William Whitaker. This is one of the few surviving images of a member of the "Williamsburg Junior Guard," later Company C, Thirty-second Virginia Infantry. Born in York County, Whitaker enlisted in 1861 at the age of eighteen and was later transferred to the "James City Cavalry."

Some companies of the Thirty-second Virginia fought in the rear-guard action outside Williamsburg on May 5, 1862, but the men of the Williamsburg Junior Guard spent the day marching in the mud toward Richmond, leaving their homes behind. It would be a long time until they returned.

Late in May 1862, Edgar Montague, a lawyer from King and Queen County, was elected colonel of the Thirty-second. The regiment fought at Seven Pines on May 31 and June 1, 1862, where the Williamsburg company received its first casualty, Private John Spraggins.

The Thirty-second Virginia Infantry served through the Seven Days' Campaign around Richmond with General Robert E. Lee's newly formed Army of Northern Virginia, participating at Savage's Station on June 29 and Malvern Hill on July 1, 1862. By September, the regiment was in Maryland at Sharpsburg. Of 158 men engaged there on September 17, 1862, the regiment suffered 72 casualties, killed and wounded, or 45 percent.

From January 1863 until the spring of 1864, the Thirty-second Virginia served in the Richmond defense lines. By this time, the entire regiment numbered about two hundred men. It fought around Richmond throughout 1864 and was present at Cold Harbor and Fort Harrison. During the last two weeks of the war, the regiment fought at Five Forks on April 1, 1865, and Sayler's Creek on April 6, where the regiment ceased to exist as a fighting force. On April 9, 1865, the Thirty-second Virginia Infantry surrendered five officers and forty-one men at Appomattox. Of these, the old Williamsburg Junior Guard surrendered three officers and six men.

Bibliography

Books, Journals, and Articles

Barziza, Decimus et Ultimus. *The Adventures of a Prisoner of War, 1863–64.* Edited by R. Anderson Shuffler. Austin, Tex.: University of Texas Press, 1964.

Battles and Leaders of the Civil War. Edited by Robert Underwood Johnson and Clarence Clough Buel. 4 vols. New York: Century, 1884–1888.

Brugger, Robert J. *Beverley Tucker: Heart over Head in the Old South.* Baltimore, Md.: Johns Hopkins University Press, 1978.

Bruton Parish Churchyard and Church: A Guide to the Tombstones, Monuments, and Mural Tablets. Williamsburg, Va.: Bruton Parish Church, 1976.

Confederate Veteran. I–XL (1893–1932).

Crute, Joseph, Jr. *Units of the Confederate States Army.* Midlothian, Va.: Derwent Books, 1987.

Cunningham, H. H. *Doctors in Gray: The Confederate Medical Service.* Baton Rouge, La.: Louisiana State University Press, 1958.

Curry, Harry Lee. *God's Rebels: Confederate Clergy in the Civil War.* Lafayette, La.: Hunting House, 1990.

Custer, George A. *Custer in the Civil War: His Unfinished Memoirs.* Compiled and edited by John M. Carroll. San Rafael, Calif.: Presidio Press, 1977.

Davis, Burke. *To Appomattox: Nine April Days, 1865.* New York: Rhinehart, 1959.

Goodwin, Rutherfoord. *A Brief & True Report Concerning Williamsburg in Virginia.* 3rd ed. Williamsburg, Va.: Colonial Williamsburg Foundation, 1972.

Hall, Richard. *Patriots in Disguise: Women Warriors of the Civil War.* New York: Paragon House, 1993.

Historical Times Illustrated Encyclopedia of the Civil War. Edited by Patricia L. Faust. New York: Harper & Row, 1986.

Jensen, Les. *32nd Virginia Infantry.* Lynchburg, Va.: H. E. Howard, 1990.

Jordon, Ervin L., Jr. *Black Confederates and Afro-Yankees in Civil War Virginia.* Charlottesville, Va.: University Press of Virginia, 1995.

Keen, Hugh C., and Horace Mewborn. *43rd Battalion Virginia Cavalry: Mosby's Command.* Lynchburg, Va.: H. E. Howard, 1993.

McClellan, George B. *McClellan's Own Story: The War for the Union. . . .* New York: C. L. Webster, 1887.

McKinney, E. P. *Life in Tent and Field, 1861–1865.* Boston: Richard G. Badger, 1922.

Milham, Charles G. *Gallant Pelham: American Extraordinary.* Washington, D. C.: Public Affairs Press, 1959.

Olmert, Michael. *Official Guide to Colonial Williamsburg.* 9th ed. Williamsburg, Va.: Colonial Williamsburg Foundation, 1995.

Parker, Sandra V. *Richmond's Civil War Prisons.* Lynchburg, Va.: H. E. Howard, 1990.

Robinson, Dale Glenwood. *The Academies of Virginia, 1776–1861.* Richmond, Va.: Dietz Press, 1977.

Rouse, Parke, Jr. *Cows on the Campus: Williamsburg in Bygone Days.* Richmond, Va.: Dietz Press, 1973.

———. *Remembering Williamsburg: A Sentimental Journey through Three Centuries.* Richmond, Va.: Dietz Press, 1989.

Sears, Stephen W. *To the Gates of Richmond: The Peninsula Campaign.* New York: Ticknor & Fields, 1992.

Tucker, Beverl[e]y Randolph. *Tales of the Tuckers: Descendants of the Main Line of St. George Tucker of Bermuda and Virginia.* Richmond, Va.: Dietz Printing, 1942.